A [illegible] Country Diary

A Welsh Country Diary

William Condry

Illustrated by Robert Gibson

GOMER

First Impression—1993

ISBN 0 86383 872 3

Printed by
J. D. Lewis & Sons Ltd., Gomer Press, Llandysul, Dyfed

Thanks are due to the Editor of *The Guardian*
for permission to use the material that makes up this book.

AUTHOR'S PREFACE

It was on 9 October, 1957 that I wrote my first 'Country Diary' for the *Manchester Guardian*. It ended with my initials, 'W.M.C.', and it was not until 1966 that my fellow country-diarists and I began to sign our offerings with our names in full. In 1961 the *Manchester Guardian* had become the *Guardian* but the country diaries carried on just as they had since someone wrote the first diary back in November, 1906. In the thirty-six years that I have been one of the diarists my first word has almost invariably been 'Machynlleth', the name of my nearest town, and so it still is.

Writing these diaries has imposed an agreeably recurring pattern on my life. No matter what else has happened, I have kept in mind the need to decide on what I hope will be a worthwhile topic and then to meet my deadline, phoning my piece to London on a Thursday and hoping that the copy-typist at the other end of a crackly line doesn't mishear anything. Though occasionally the spelling of Welsh place-names defeats the copy-typists I never cease to wonder at their skill and speed; and sometimes they have entered into the spirit of the moment and offered approving comments or even suggested a better word here and there. I am grateful also to the features editors for their unfailing helpfulness.

Another of the many rewards of writing these diaries has been to receive so many friendly letters from *Guardian* readers. Or they phone to tell me they have just seen a hoopoe in their garden or heard a golden oriole. Other readers have exchanged greetings when I have given talks at natural history societies, making me feel I belong to a widespread club of like-minded people. And as the *Guardian* circulates worldwide as a weekly, I occasionally get letters from places I have never heard of on the other side of the globe.

The three hundred and fifty or so diaries that make up this book are intended as a representative selection of the subjects I have written about over the years. Some are straight natural history. Many are concerned with conservation or other countryside problems. Others, by touching on past events, may have some historical interest. All, I hope, will speak to somebody, somewhere.

CONTENTS

JANUARY

Silent Spring, 1963

If you are looking for stimulating ideas on the link between food and health you will find them in the current number of that excellent quarterly, *Mother Earth, the* journal of the Soil Association. There are several cautionary articles on the dangers of using pesticides and chemical fertilisers. (In Australia insecticides caused schizophrenia as well as physical breakdown in workers in orchards.) These articles leave me more than ever alarmed by the scientists' excessive confidence in the safety of their chemicals when, in fact, so little is really known about the true as distinguished from the guessed-at safety levels of any chemical doses.

And so we come to *Silent Spring,* by Rachel Carson, excellently reviewed in *Mother Earth.* This book will, we pray, be a best-seller in Britain as it is in America. The silence of Rachel Carson's spring is the silence that will come to the world when we have killed off all the singing birds with insecticides. It is a silence that symbolises all the horrifying effects on nature and on ourselves by the mass onslaught by poison that man is now launching on the earth. So far we have seen only a shadow of what could come unless the reckless madness that has got into our scientists, our agriculturists, our horticulturists and our forestry experts is checked pretty soon.

Consider the Lilies

An old man lived in a cottage on a bend of the winding hill. He had a garden which he loved, and no wonder for it grew madonna lilies as few gardens will. They spread wildly into every corner of that garden and in summer they filled it from hedge to hedge with their fragrant white trumpets. Once he gave us a few of the bulbs but in our garden they failed. We always intended going back to ask for more, but passing one day we noticed the cottage was empty. The old chap would grow no more lilies. We went away hoping the place would fall into the hands of someone who would care for the lilies. Instead, the authorities seized the chance of demolishing the cottage in order to take the bend out of the road. They would claim they are getting rid of a dangerous corner. But I wonder if we are really any better off?

I know we are not allowed to say in a voice louder than a whisper that speed is a major cause of accidents. So when the traffic comes down the hill faster than ever we shall be expected to applaud and say this is progress. But all I can see is that we have exchanged a garden beautiful with lilies for a dull roadside bank. And drivers can now go racing into the next bend even more recklessly than they could before.

A House far from Anywhere, 1961

A house near here is called, aptly enough, Plas y Mynydd (The Mountain House). It stands at a lake-side in a remote hollow of the moorland, 1,300 feet above sea-level. It is somewhat sheltered on the west by trees but it has no protection against the east winds that come at if from the ridges of Pumlumon. It is a lonely house. Wide empty hills stretch all about, and for neighbours you must go three miles north, four miles south, two miles west or seven miles east. And if you went off south-east you would walk all day before you saw smoke in a chimney.

Not that this Plas y Mynydd has always been so neighbourless. When it was built there were little occupied crofts (*tyddynnod*) scattered about the hills. All these are gone now except for a few crumbling walls and are only names in the memory of far off village folk who got them from their parents and grandparents.

The *tyddynod* were poorly built and once abandoned they quickly rotted in the moorland rains. But Plas y Mynydd was bigger and stronger and has been occupied until recently. But now its time, too, is up. Already its back wall has fallen to the grass and very soon it will be nothing more than a grassy mound for the passer-by to wonder at. And there will be no house at all in all those miles of hills.

A Luckless Welsh House, 1960

Not long ago I received a picture-postcard from a friend which shows a photograph of Hafod, once one of Cardiganshire's best-known houses. The card is cheerlessly entitled: 'Hafod, a Centre of Great Misfortunes'. It shows the mansion as it was some thirty years ago (it was destroyed by fire in 1807, rebuilt by 1810, but is now demolished). It also shows the man who twice built it, Thomas Johnes, as Chantrey sculptured him at his daughter's death-bed. (The sculpture was lost in a fire at Hafod church in 1932.)

The misfortunes of this romantic spendthrift, scholar and pioneer agriculturist have often been recounted. But what fewer people remember is that in that fire of 1807 were lost the manuscripts of the greatest Welsh naturalist and archaeologist of his day, Edward Lhuyd, who died in 1709. These voluminous papers were the rough notes of Lhuyd's projected great work on the history, geography and natural history of Wales. True, only half Lhuyd's papers went to Hafod. But though the collection was divided most of the rest was equally doomed, being lost in a fire at a bookbinder's shop in London.

What a wonderfully valuable record these natural history notes would be to us today had they survived. For Lhuyd was knowledgeable about everything: birds, insects, shells and, above all, plants and fossils. Yes, there is no doubt of it: the misfortunes of Hafod were great indeed.

A Memorial Fit for a King

On a fine morning recently I found myself sitting on a grassy bank near the Welsh border facing a magnificent view of the mountains of north Wales. I had climbed this rampart without curiosity, simply to get a high perch on which to eat my lunch. Then seeing that it stretched far on either hand I realised that I had happened upon a section of Offa's Dyke. How frequently this occurs along the Border, this chance falling in with the Dyke. It is like meeting an old friend. But a very changeable friend: for after a dozen centuries it is much better preserved in some places than others. Near where I sat a cart-track had gone clean through it, leaving walls on either side that were about twice my height. But a cart-track is only a pin-prick compared with what has happened to the Dyke elsewhere. Often it vanishes altogether from the scene or is only a swelling wave across ploughland or a mere bump in a country road.

Happily the Dyke belongs essentially to the hills, where the need to level it has been much less. So it is on the high ground that you see it at its finest, massively breasting steep slopes and looking defiance towards the west. Only an earthen bank but transformed by the centuries into something altogether beautiful. What more lasting memorial could any king have?

Mysterious Old Dykes

Last summer I walked a little way along the fragmentary Pembrokeshire earthwork called Monk's Dyke which stretches for some four miles across St David's peninsula. I like to think of the long endurance of these simple banks and ditches. This one was built maybe thirteen centuries ago to mark off the tip of the peninsula as a domain of Celtic monks. There is, I think, a greater fascination about these earthworks of the Dark Ages even than about, say, the far more ancient Hadrian's Wall, simply because we know so much less about them. Take Offa's Dyke, which goes across 120 miles of hillsides and valleys. Archaeologists have told us how it is constructed but we know almost nothing of its history.

We know far less about numerous other dykes scattered about Britain. In Wales there is Wat's Dyke near the north end of Offa's Dyke; snatches of earthworks on Kerry Hill in Montgomeryshire and others in Radnorshire; and south of these is the Great Dyke on high ground in Carmarthenshire. In Somerset are the sixty miles of the famous Wansdyke. But who was Wan (if he existed) and when and why should anyone want a dyke just there? But these unanswered questions are how things should be. For one of the many strange polarities in man's nature is that while he wants everything explained (hence the sciences), he likes at the same time to feel surrounded by mysteries (hence the religions).

The Man who loved Curlews

A man I used to know had a passion for curlews. His house overlooked the estuary of the Dyfi river so closely that the tide washed against his garden wall, and curlews were his constant neighbours. He saw other creatures too. Sometimes with the tide came grebes, divers, mergansers or big leaping fish with porpoises or grey seals after them. And when the tide ebbed off the mud-flats he would watch the wader flocks gather for the worm-harvest. Sometimes he slept badly and would lie awake listening to the estuary: the gentle lap-lapping of a neap-tide under his wall; or the urgent hissing and gurgling of the great springs. But on some nights even the estuary would be quite without sound, the whole vast expanse of mud and water lying in absolute silence through the sleepless hours.

But sooner or later, lying there he would be sure to hear the deep wailings and liquid bubblings of the curlews and this gave him intense delight. When he died he left behind several scrapbooks in which he had collected a mass of curlew lore; poems and bits of prose clipped out of innumerable books and magazines, every one of them about curlews. And now I live near the estuary and at times I wake in the night and hear the curlews crying in the darkness. Then I remember my old friend.

Shepherd of the Hills

To go and see Jenkins is to go back a century. You let the winding track lift you up amid wind and rocks and heather and from there you look back to the lowlands as to a foreign country. You round a last bend in the lane and there is the lonely farmhouse under the snowy slopes of the mountain. And here, greeting you in the lane, stands a primitive figure. On his head an ancient hat once worn by his mother when in her eighties she worked on top of the hay loads. Round his shoulders a sack pinned at his breast by a four-inch nail. Under the sack a policeman's tunic bought for a few pence at Machynlleth mart.

Jenkins is ageing now but still very strong. His face is furrowed by long exposure. His eyes have grown smaller. His lips are chapped by frost. His character has gone as hard as the rocks. He lives alone now in the cold, comfortless house, though he is reputedly wealthy. So he always has lived and all his people. And so he will go on living. 'Not softly in hot-houses down there,' he says, looking with contempt to the valley. No, he will live hardily, mostly out-of-doors with the sheep; doctoring himself, if ever he has to, by his own herbs. So, he claims, he will still be well and active when the years have gathered thickly about him. I believe he will.

Harriers over the Winter Marshes

Of all the birds that fly over the winter estuary none is finer than the male hen harrier. But I think the picture in the books do him little justice. They make him look too subdued, too blue-grey, not striking enough. For in the sunshine he is white and conspicuous, with boldly contrasting black wing tips, an altogether fascinating bird as he comes on long-winged and leisurely flight low across the saltings. Often he drops into ditches and creeks, quickly rising again for he rarely seems to catch anything. Crowds of curlews and wigeon rise in anxiety as he passes but their fears seem groundless for his preferred prey is usually much smaller fowl.

There is a female hen harrier here also, so different in her dark-brown plumage as to seem a quite different species. But though I see one or the other nearly every day I never see them together, for harriers in winter are strictly individualists. Sometimes they fly close to me, turning to look at me with total indifference, without either fear or even curiosity. Then on they go, rising high over woods and hills to marshes miles away, as if they were off on far migrations. Yet I know they will return. In two or three hours, or may be not till tomorrow, they will come to hunt here again and cause another flutter of panic among the birds of the estuary.

Machynlleth for Floods

The house in which my wife and I live has a long history. A document in the National Library of Wales, Aberystwyth, refers to it in 1680, but it could well be much older. And there could have been earlier houses on the spot. Whoever they were who first chose to live here, they clearly knew what they were doing. So close to the estuary and surrounded as it then was by wide marshland, this must have looked a rather unpromising spot for a home. But last week, as the waters rose and cut us off, we were grateful to those who cunningly placed this house just above the level of the floods. Less happy were those whose houses were invaded by the river and saw their carpets and furniture ruined. This is an area that is quite used to being swamped and as the waters spread out last week to form a lake about seven miles long, there was the usual reminiscing about the inundations of previous years and we had the inevitable discussions about which flood rose the highest. In the end the greybeards have to win these arguments. They can always remember floods a yard deeper than anybody else, and how can the younger ones really challenge such claims? No doubt this latest flood will go on getting deeper in people's memories and in due course will have become the worst in living memory like all the others. Misery though it was for many of us, the flood had its lighter side as the BBC London news-readers kept on repeating a ridiculously exaggerated report about a local village being evacuated. But best of all was hearing them trying to say 'Machynlleth'.

A Peaty Wilderness

I write this looking across the great peatbog that lies behind the Cardiganshire coast at Borth. Many have been the attempts to drain this great morass, but although agriculture has nibbled round its margins, its centre, raised like the crown on a bowling green, remains inviolate. No doubt to some, farmers especially, who see this wilderness, it is a disgraceful waste of land that ought to be put to 'better' use. But to many people, including those farmers with poetry in their hearts (there is no shortage of such in Wales), the survival of this great bog is a tonic to the spirit. They look across it on a sunny day and see the cloud shadows playing over the coloured zones of vegetation, the pale-green reed beds, the white spreads of cotton grass, the dark-brown heather, the grey-green willow thickets, and they are glad it is now safeguarded as a National Nature Reserve. In Welsh it is called Cors Fochno, a name that could have come to us from the remotest past. Perhaps the Celts of 4,000 years ago, when they were still living in Eastern Europe, had names like this for the vast peatbogs of the Danube. People no doubt years ago were afraid of a great mire like Cors Fochno. But we, in this drainage-mad age, have learned to love it. For it is not only beautiful, it is almost the only one left.

Island of Saints and Birds

You could be forgiven if you have never heard of Aberdaron. It is the last little village along the Llŷn peninsula, north-west Wales, and is best known for its medieval church on the edge of the sea. Here for centuries pilgrims said their final prayers (or had prayers said over their bodies) before going across to Bardsey (Ynys Enlli), a holy island two miles beyond the last headland. Not long after the war I first set foot on Bardsey and found the place so appealing I could have stayed there for years. Instead, I did the next best thing. I joined a group of friends in taking a lease of one of the island's houses, and this we made into an observatory where birdwatchers and other naturalists could stay at minimum cost by catering for themselves. Now, forty years later, I am happy to report that the observatory is still alive and well. Living conditions are not quite as primitive as they used to be, but on the whole the observatory, like Bardsey itself, is happily unmodernised. So if you enjoy the wildlife of land and sea; or if bird-ringing appeals to you; and if you can live for a while close to the elements, and if you would not be broken in spirit if you were delayed on the island by gales, then Bardsey could be the place for your next holiday.

Mining Threats in National Parks in the 1970s

If the only thing at stake in Rio Tinto Zinc's menace to Snowdonia were the opencast mining of one huge site alone, this would be bad enough. But there is much more to it than that. What about those other companies waiting on the touch-line to see how RTZ gets on? And RTZ themselves are not going to be content with just this one concession. They are reported as seeking to prospect such delectable regions as the Beddgelert country and also Cwm Pennant, a valley near Cricieth famous for its beauty. So the Snowdonia National Park is threatened from north to south because its rocks far and wide are full of exploitable minerals. The economic arguments in favour of all this mining may be very strong. But so are the non-economic arguments against. We are up against the old problem. How can we evaluate beautiful landscapes, unpolluted air and water and the enormous benefits people get from such priceless assets? Recently the Prime Minister declared: 'The protection of our countryside and the prevention of pollution are among the highest priorities of the seventies. It is in this spirit that the Government will tackle the problem . . .' Good. Let them begin by protecting Snowdonia. If they refuse, then let them tell us what National Parks are for and also where people should go for a holiday in unspoilt scenery and an unpolluted environment.

Double Standards in European Conservation Year, 1970

Undoubtedly European Conservation Year is the year in which we British really ought to try not to be such hypocrites about nature conservation. Take birds. Our record in bird protection at home is excellent. Apart from a few nasty birds and some that have the misfortune to be classed as fair game, all our birds are protected by stringent laws. Yet we quite happily take advantage of the fact that other countries fail to protect their birds: we allow our cage-bird industry to import thousands of birds annually from all over the world. And it's the same with animals. What is worse, we know full well that for every animal or bird that gets here alive a vast number die in being caught or transported. Similarly with plants. We have many local laws forbidding the uprooting of our wildflowers. Yet botanists and gardeners who would never uproot a choice British plant will quite cheerfully come home from abroad with a load of exquisite foreign plants. One horticultural journal recently had an article describing how a score of British gardening enthusiasts pillaged their way through the wild flora of another country. Joyously the author related how they collected a large number of plants wherever they went, their delight culminating in the final triumph when 'the Customs allowed us through each with our plastic bags containing the spoils of a truly enjoyable tour'. We must learn to be better Europeans than that.

Owl Homes—Made in Birmingham

Today two men, lurching under a load of heavy boxes, are splashing across the marshes to the pine wood. They are followed by a little girl, daughter of one of them. She carries a coil of rope. Her father has devoted the spare time of several weeks to demolishing an old hen-coop and using the wood to make the boxes which they have brought a hundred miles from the industrial Midlands, setting off early so as to have a good long day in this wood near the coast of Wales. Carefully they examine the trees, choosing those best fitted for their purpose. Then high up each tree one of them climbs, lowers the rope, and a box is attached to it. He hauls it up, sites it on the shady side of the trunk and fixes it firmly there. So the day goes on and their burden gets lighter as box after box finds a home in a tree-top. By tea-time they have finished. The light is fading as they get into their car and roar off back towards the Midlands, happy in a day well spent. I dare say their workmates would consider that climbing about tree-tops all day is a very singular way of spending a Sunday. But each to his taste. And perhaps all her life the little girl will remember the day she spent in a Welsh wood helping to provide homes for owls and kestrels.

Wildlife Unafraid of Vehicles

When I pulled into a layby yesterday a rabbit was soon grazing fearlessly a few feet away. Yet a harmless little chaffinch suddenly arriving with a flurry of wings sent the rabbit off in a panic. To wildlife the cost of this failure to understand that cars contain people has been colossal. Animals and birds throughout the world, especially those on plains, have been decimated by hunters shooting from vehicles. You might expect that the very noises peculiar to modern man would panic all wild creatures. But not at all. A few years ago an owl nested in a factory wall with a heavy machine thundering right next to it. In such circumstances, is there some defence mechanism that switches off the hearing power of ears that can hear the rustle of mice in grass from many yards distance? Which reminds me of an encounter I had with a buzzard. This bird was perched on a bough twenty-five feet above the road but when I stopped my car beneath him he did not fly off. As an experiment I pipped my horn very gently. No reaction. A bit louder. Same result. So I gave him quite a blast. Still no sign he had heard. And even when I kept my finger down for as long as I could bear the din the buzzard remained indifferent. But as soon as I opened the car door half an inch he had gone.

Growing Pollution Awareness, 1970

So 1970 comes and DDT begins to go. It is a promising start for a special conservation year. If DDT conquered malaria somewhere, then all credit to it. But now that we have non-persistent insecticides that will do the job, let us shed no tears over DDT and all other unpleasant substances that have been showered wholesale on fields and forests, poisoning everything within range, and have then been washed into the rivers killing fish and fish-eating eagles and so down to the sea, until the farthest limits of the ocean and its animals are now polluted. What a fantastic degree of pollution the world accepts before doing anything about it! The totally dead Lake Erie, 10,000 square miles of it: most people who live by it apparently accept its death as an inevitable part of progress. This attitude is at the heart of the matter. If was the nineteenth-century champions of progress who convinced the western world that it was heading towards its 'manifest destiny'. This is the philosophy that has persuaded the twentieth century to believe that all scientific and technological progress is good for us. Dissenting voices from Thoreau onwards were for a long time few and scarcely heard. Thoreau said: 'They may go their way to their manifest destiny which I trust is not mine'. Now, suddenly, the world is full of Thoreaus. Everyone talks of pollution not progress. May they keep it up, loud and clear.

Exit the Red Squirrel

I can hardly believe it, because my memories are still so vivid, but come this summer it will be all of 20 years since I last saw red squirrels hereabouts. I remember also what an agony it was to see the lovely red ones disappearing and the not so lovely grey ones taking their place. The first greys were seen here in late December, 1952. Not the nicest of Christmas presents, we thought. But for as much as seven years they remained quite shy and scarce. Then they began to increase and quite suddenly, in 1961, everybody was reporting them in woods and gardens, along the roads, even on the promenade at Aberystwyth. This it seems was the pattern in many districts as these Americans spread through the land, stealthily consolidating their position for several years, then quite abruptly changing their life-style and becoming the bold and obvious creatures we know today. A note I made on 16 June, 1963, reads very sadly now: 'Today I saw a red squirrel in the pine wood. It is the third this week so maybe they are increasing'. So much for the optimism of a fine summer morning. The reality was that I never saw or heard of another from that day on. After ten years of struggle the red squirrel had finally given up a place it had occupied perhaps since the post-glacial forests first crept across Britain. But, if mother nature can produce one quirk maybe she can manage another. She may have ousted the red squirrel today but in another twenty years who knows?

Look Out for Pillow Mounds, 1984

A gap in my education was filled this week when I visited the offices of the Royal Commission on Ancient Monuments in Aberystwyth and heard all about the history of rabbit farming. It may seem incredible to present-day farmers, accustomed to regard the rabbit as a major pest, that until well into the last century it was a carefully farmed animal that in the wild was rather uncommon. A native of southern Europe, the rabbit was brought to Britain by the Normans and kept in enclosures guarded by warreners. At some stage the practice arose of building mounds, usually in groups, in which rabbits could burrow more easily than into hard level ground. Large numbers of these mounds had been built in many parts of Britain by the time rabbit farming finally ceased. After that their purpose was quickly forgotten. Understandably, since they have some slight resemblance to Neolithic burial mounds, they were at first regarded with interest by archaeologists who called them pillow mounds but had no idea of their origin and purpose. It must have been a great disappointment when it was eventually realised that this distinctive and numerous class of earthwork contained mere rabbit warrens. Though they lack the glamour of ancient burial chambers these pillow mounds are part of our history and deserve to be properly studied and recorded before they all disappear, destroyed by farming, forestry and other activities. No doubt a great many still await discovery, especially in the wilder parts of the countryside. So we need to keep our eyes open next time we head for the uplands.

Opportunist Squirrel

Salt marshes, those wide areas of mud and grassland especially characteristic of estuaries and low-lying coasts, are famous for birds but what about their mammals? At first sight they hardly look promising for mammals for although the ground is honeycombed with lovely holes and tunnels these are all frequently flooded by the tides. So on the saltings we find no hole dwellers such as rodents or rabbits, moles or shrews. But the opportunists come, those that can cover plenty of ground in a short time and have the wit to retreat before quickly advancing waters. Foxes particularly, judging by their footprints in the snow, must often venture across the saltings on winter nights in pursuit of roosting water birds. And sometimes we see mammals out there by day, especially hares. Once a stoat came swimming across the river. Though mobbed by yodelling redshanks and dived at by outraged shelducks, he hunted calmly over the grassland in broadest daylight, no doubt hoping to collect some unsuspecting bird. But the most unexpected animal I ever saw on the saltings was a grey squirrel. Flushed by a spaniel from long grass far out in the estuary, the squirrel looked round for a tree to climb, but seeing none in sight, rushed up the dog-owner's body as the next best thing and stood on the astonished man's head. So resourceful a species deserves success, don't you think?

Time-honoured Bird Names

In one of our local conifer forests I met an elderly man with a pair of binoculars. He was bird-watching, he said, and had just been observing some golden-crested wrens. I was delighted. Not because he had seen a party of goldcrests, for I knew they were there, but because he had called them golden crested wrens. I like all these old bird names and it seems a pity to let them die out. So I say long live names like dabchick, hedge sparrow, willow wren and others I was brought up with. I would even revive those my father knew when he was a lad. For him a chaffinch was always a pie-finch, a goldfinch was a seven-coloured linnet and a yellowhammer was never anything but a scribbling schoolmaster. Now I hear there is a move afoot to invent a whole new set of English names for birds. Well that's all right provided they are not going to try and force the rest of us to use them. Some years ago the botanists tried to standardise the English names of wild flowers, but while many of their suggestions were sensible enough, others were rather whimsical and I just could not bring myself to adopt them. One of the glories of the English language is its marvellous wealth of vocabulary, and therefore we must not allow ourselves to be straight-jacketed into always using just one name for a plant or an animal when, if you include the dialect names, there may be a dozen to choose from. So ends my sermon. I'm off up the river now in the hope of seeing a water ouzel or maybe even a peggy dishwasher.

Stoats on the Bird-table

Until this week I had never been much of a stoat-watcher, but suddenly I have become quite an addict. It all began when we saw a stoat running across our garden (stoats always seem to run rather than walk), and what a striking animal it was! Instead of having the usual reddish-brown back, it was a very pale pink. Its shoulders were conspicuously white and so was its long tail, except for the black tip. It came again next day and amazed us by climbing up the bird-table to eat peanuts with such ease of manner that it might have done this every day of its life. On the third day we had another surprise when a different stoat, one in normal brown pelage, came and helped itself to the peanuts. Since then both stoats have returned to the bird-table but never together. The question that naturally arises is why should we have had a bird-table for thirty years without ever seeing a stoat on it, and now, suddenly, have two as regular visitors. The answer may lie in those peanuts. For they were given to us by a friend of ours who had mixed them in various meat and poultry fats. So, presumably, when these carnivorous stoats are crunching those tasty nuts, they think they are eating the bones of animals. Perhaps I ought to add that no one need fear that a stoat turning white or partly white in winter is a portent of hard weather. In fact, the records show that a few stoats may turn white even in the south of England in any year, regardless of the weather.

An Alien Plant on Snowdon, 1987

I remember years ago an eminent English bird expert making a rather imprudent suggestion. His idea was that because so few British birds breed in the Forestry Commission's plantations of North American spruces, we might liven things up by introducing some of the American birds which live in natural forests of this kind. The proposal was coldly received. Biologists are, after all, always warning us about the folly of bringing in alien species. Once I was with a party of botanists in the sand-dunes at Harlech when we came upon a single young plant of sea buckthorn. Our leader immediately destroyed it, because this prickly bush is alien to Wales and can soon spread into impenetrable thickets, smothering all other vegetation. I happen at present to be planning my usual few summer days of botanising in the mountains of north Wales. And a plant which comes to mind is an alpine called *Ramonda*, the leaves of which I saw on Snowdon last summer. *Ramonda* is not a British native. It is well-known in gardens but in the wild it grows no nearer than the Pyrenees. With other exotic alpines, it was planted on Snowdon as an experiment about fifty years ago, to the consternation of most botanists. They need not have worried. Snowdon's sheep and Snowdon's weather soon put paid to the lot, except for two or three poor lingering ramondas which rarely produce a flower. Could 1987, I wonder, bring us one of those special summers when even a Snowdon *Ramonda* will give us one of its lovely pale-mauve blooms? And if so, should we rejoice in it, or tear it up by the roots?

Spying out Harvest Mice

Are you familiar with the plant called purple moorgrass? It is the tall grass of marshy ground that makes those big awkward tussocks that cause people to stumble all over the place and get all hot and bad-tempered. Yet even the clumpiest moorgrass has its virtues, as a friend and I found out on Wednesday morning. We had been urged to look out for Britain's smallest rodent, the harvest mouse. In much of England and Wales this tiny mammal has long been regarded as absent but recent fieldwork has suggested that it may be more widespread than had been supposed. Because it is so shy, minute and almost nocturnal, it is seldom seen. Nor is it easy to trap. So to prove its presence all you can really do is find its nests. And this is where moorgrass comes in. The harvest mouse, which lives in marshes as much as in cornfields, just loves to place its little ball of a nest in the heart of the moorgrass tussocks. So we set out to search our local marsh though we had no reason whatever to believe there might be harvest mice there. But naturalists live by optimism and, hey presto, the very first clump we examined had an old harvest mouse nest in its heart. So my advice to anyone thinking of walking across a moorgrass bog is: don't do anything so exhausting but look for harvest mice instead. It's far more rewarding.

Strange Life-style of the Woodcock

The cold weather this week has brought us that bird of mystery, the woodcock. This nonconformist member of the wader tribe lies all day so invisible on the woodland floor that I have never yet spotted one before it has spotted me and gone swerving away through the trees. Woodcock are emphatically loners. You may flush many in an hour or two but nearly always one at a time and it is only in the severest weather that I have ever known them to gather into what was almost a flock. My memory goes back to the great snows of early 1947, when blizzards drove countless woodcock from more eastern districts into what they hoped would be the milder west. In the event, it was snowier here than anywhere else and the woodcock were soon starving and weak. In desperation they found their way in hundreds to the rough slopes above the sea cliffs where the ground was less frozen. But even there many perished. Each year when spring comes the woodcock are early to nest but sadly very few breed in this part of Wales. Here and there, however, we can watch the curious evening flight of the males who make slow circuits round the woods, alternately croaking and squeaking. They have another strange habit. When danger threatens, an adult woodcock can pick up its young between its legs and airlift it to safety. I confess that for years I doubted if it were possible; then one season I saw the trick performed twice within a few days. I felt duly chastened and now I try to keep a more open mind about the countless old wives' tales of natural history.

A Box of Curios

Having a horror of getting cluttered up with useless possessions I was possibly a little less than grateful when, some time ago, a revered friend presented me with a box of curios. Its contents were: some sea shells of delicate intricacy; bits of pumice labelled 'Pompeii, 1903'; some colourful baubles described as 'mosaics from St Paul's Cathedral'; a pinch of 'drift weed from the Gulf Stream off the coast of Africa, December, 1871' (and after ninety years still faintly ocean-scented); 15 amethyst-hued mollusc shells accompanying the drift weed; chips of pink rock labelled 'Forum', 'Colosseum' and 'Palatine Hill'; some brown nodules which are 'earth from the catacombs at Rome'; three little dried-up sea-horses with long curly tails; assorted modern foreign coins; and finally one ancient Greek coin from Paestum.

Curios being the quintessence of uselessness, I ought to have passed this collection on. So why haven't I? I think it is because of that one Greek coin (which is so tiny I would certainly lose it if I did not keep the whole box). This coin must be well over two-thousand years old, yet the name on it and the designs of Poseidon's head and of Eros on a dolphin, though faint, are still beautiful. Holding it in my hand I have immediate physical contact, however infinitesimal, with something wonderful: I mean the art, the skill, the knowledge they had in Greece when here, at the other end of Europe, life was still so very, very primitive.

FEBRUARY

Railway Memories, 1963

They grumbled, yes, I'm sure they grumbled, at all the railways being built through the countryside a century ago. You can imagine the bitter things they said about peace and beauty being annihilated. And of course they were justified where railways brought industrialisation. But even Britain's little countryside is surprisingly big. You can hurt it—new towns, power stations, caravan sites hurt it abominably—but it can absorb much else without harm. And it has certainly absorbed many a railway.

Take that line down the Welsh Wye from Rhayader. It goes with the river along one of the loveliest valleys in Europe, yet is quite unobtrusive. It has become a part of the scene. In fact, the trains on it are rather a novelty to see unexpectedly bursting out of the woods in such a wild place.

But on that line the passenger service has now finished, as it will very soon on those many delectable routes that one day will be something for the aged to reminisce about. And if at some future date I shall look back nostalgically to former railways, I shall speak with most regret of the little trains that used to take us in spring up the greening woods of Wyre, up from the Severn and down to the Teme into an enchanted land where the line ran through miles of cherry trees in blossom and ended at a little rustic station called Woofferton.

To Rome—by Welsh Rail

Palimpsest—that was the word I wanted recently when I stood on Caersws station in central Montgomeryshire. For what I saw in an adjacent field reminded me that it was not only a platform I was standing on but also (though I've only just thought of the word) a palimpsest. At school they told us this strangely shaped word meant an erased manuscript that had been used for other writings. But I do not recall that they ever tried to quicken our imagination by showing us the living palimpsest of the earth's face all about us. True they took us round an occasional castle or cathedral, things huge and remote from our everyday experience. But I think we would have felt a more vivid appeal from something nearer to earth, even mere lines and banks faintly traceable in fields and dimly suggesting old roads and former habitations. A place like Caersws station, for instance.

For here at the side of the platform lie straight banks that have survived some 1,700 years, the banks of a Roman fort which not even a railway station has succeeded in obliterating. Such was the vandalism of the railway age. Today we expect, though do not always receive, better treatment for our ancient monuments. Happily at the next Roman camp west of Caersws, half-way up Plynlimon Pass, the Forestry Commission has perforce left the site unplanted as an open space amid the conifers.

The Lady with the Oxford Degree

The lady with the Oxford degree looked across to the hills. 'The high one,' she said, 'is called Mynydd Mawr. We went up there last summer. There's nothing of interest.' Then she went on with her dazzling conversation about Sartre and existentialism until none of us had any doubt that she was very well read in French literature. My own regret was that she had not read a little more English. She might then have met that poem about ships in bottles that D. H. Lawrence wrote especially for the likes of her. But would she have even seen the point of it? Certainly I could not see the point of all this learning if it left people unable to appreciate places like Mynydd Mawr.

For in summer on Mynydd Mawr the larks sing like heaven. Ravens and buzzards soar beautifully overhead, ring ouzels pipe from the rocks, blackcock bubble and leap among the heather. On Mynydd Mawr there are sheets of the lovely mossy saxifrage and there is roseroot there, starry saxifrage, mountain sorrel, oak fern and ledges yellow with globe-flowers. But perhaps this hill is most notable for its traces of ancient man: on the summit a line of noble cairns; on the slopes many hut-circles and cromlechs; everywhere the remains of the lives of simple people. I wonder what the lady with the Oxford degree expected to find up there. A reading party, perhaps, or a few volumes of Proust?

Whimsies of the Mountain Weather

Who shall foretell the vagaries of our western weather? Last Saturday a friend and I met in Dolgellau to go for a mountain walk. When we felt the knives and daggers the east wind was hurling through the streets we wondered what agonies awaited us on the tops. We struck off on foot towards the north-east under a cold blue sky; but a murky greyness hid the distant hills. Yet we had not walked more than an hour when, to our astonishment, clouds began to build up from the west. Quite abruptly the east wind lost its sting and died altogether. Incredibly, in the deep valley under the rocks of Craig y Benglog, we ate our lunch in the heat, and I mean the heat, of the February sun.

Then we climbed the flanks of Rhobell Fawr, first across half-frozen marshes, then up ringing grassy slopes and finally scrambling over screes and snow-drifts. As we got higher we began to feel again the gust and snatch of a great wind. But this wind carried no arms. It was a kindly wind from the sea that dispelled the murk and gave us from the top a view as far as Cnicht. Yet as we descended, rejoicing in the warmer air, the weather was preparing another frolic and by the time we were back in Dolgellau an icy-fingered wind had already struck again from the east.

Mountain on a Once Troubled Border

The Long Mountain near Welshpool is one of 'those blue remembered hills' I have looked up to for years from the main Shrewsbury road and always been hurrying somewhere else, and it was not until last weekend that through the hospitality of friends I was able to get there at last. It is no ordinary mountain (as my car engine, though used to Welsh climbs, immediately told me by boiling on the way up). It is one of those places that are singularly rich in traces of man's past. On the top are a tumulus and two camps, one of which (the Beacon Ring) is particularly fine. In ancient times a very direct road ran right along the mountain to link east with west.

Offa's Dyke, so fond of western slopes, naturally passed along the western end of Long Mountain. Then in the Middle Ages the abbey of Strata Marcella used this mountain as sheep pasture: of which the farm named Monksfields still reminds us. There is a castle (or rather the last traces of one); and if you like old battlefields you will find several to keep you happy. I like less deathly associations and prefer to remember the long years of Old Parr who breathed the air of this place for a century and a half, if his story was true. I do hope it was.

The Impenetrable Forest, 1960

Old woodlands develop a personality. I am thinking especially of one near here which we privately call the Impenetrable Forest. It is a wood of pines rooted in waterlogged peaty ground. Try to enter this wood and you find yourself confronted everywhere by a twenty-foot green wall of rhododendrons extending solidly far into the pines.

It is a place full of the strong wild reek of foxes. And so safe do they feel among those fast thickets that you can walk outside the wood and hear them barking nonchalantly in broad daylight, or in what passes for broad daylight in the green glooms deep in the trees.

We call it impenetrable but, in fact, it is just possible to get right into the heart of this wood. But your back must be supple and your determination strong. For your only way is the fox's way. You must slide there with stealth along secret ways; not through but beneath all that welter of undergrowth, along old half-filled ditches that are the relics of former drainages. And should you do this you will be rewarded by a pleasant little surprise. For in the very centre of this wood, quite unexpectedly, you see the sky again and step out into a clearing, a place of quite wonderful stillness and seclusion, with a dreamlike 'Pelléas et Mélisande' sort of atmosphere about it. But after a while you may begin to feel a but uneasy about finding your way out again.

Sunday as it was in Wales

You may or may not have heard of the Reverend Griffith Jones, the bicentenary of whose death falls this year (1961). Yet his was one of the truly reforming and original minds of the eighteenth century. At a time when there was practically no popular education in Wales and when the status of the Welsh language could not have been lower, he took education (by his invention of the travelling school whose medium was Welsh) to thousands whom hardly anyone else thought worth trying to educate. The fact that a great deal of the uncouthness of the eighteenth century was not handed on to the nineteenth was largely due to such pioneers.

He was, for instance, one of the reformers of that riotous and rumbustious institution, the eighteenth-century Sunday, though in inventing the nineteenth-century Welsh sabbath perhaps he did go a bit far. Here, for instance, is a contemporary list of Sunday 'vices' for the abolition of which he was given much of the credit: 'Those savage sports and idle amusements by which the sabbath was formerly profaned, such as bull-baiting, cock-fighting, skittles and other species of gambling, wrestling, cudgel-fencing, and fighting, dancing, kicking football, playing on the harp and violin, profane swearing, &c. . . . it was not unusual in Wales for a clergyman to sit on the churchyard wall on a summer's afternoon after prayers and play on the violin for the amusement of his flock while they were dancing on the green.' What a pity this last custom has gone!

The Barmouth Fern Lives On

Last century, when there was a craze for collecting ferns, people used to flock into Wales in pursuit of specimens. Tourist literature sometimes gave advice about the best fern-hunting localities. And among these likely spots were the hills above Barmouth where, the guide books said, you might find the little lanceolate spleenwort which some collectors called the Barmouth fern. Finding myself in Barmouth one morning I remembered that advice and decided to go and look for this fern, though, for all I knew, the Victorians might have cleaned it up long ago. My pocket guide to wild flowers informed me that this fern 'has a curious predilection for old mineshafts' which sounded really adventurous. Off I went to inspect the abandoned mines above the town. But though I searched and searched those mines my efforts were all in vain. It was a shining day, the mountain tops beckoned, I lost all interest in botany and had a very good day walking the hills instead. The setting sun was already in my eyes as I began the long descent from the uplands and it was early dusk when I came down the last steep lane into Barmouth. It was then I noticed a bright-green fern in one of the walls. But now I was tired, my brain much slower than my eye, and I walked on forty yards before I told myself that there had been something different about that little fern. So I turned back and it was well that I did so because soon I was able to go on my way rejoicing that despite the Victorian predators the Barmouth fern lives on.

Preserve the Last Wild Places! 1984

Here we live between two famous mountains, Pumlumon and Cader Idris. Pumlumon is a vast bulge of wild moorland now threatened by a deplorable scheme to improve it for farming. Cader Idris in contrast is higher and rockier and is, or should be, protected by being in a national park. But even Cader has recently suffered. One of its flanks has been horribly scarred by new farm roads which run up the slopes and can be seen as eyesores from far away. The fact is that if you are a farmer, you are no ordinary mortal. Without planning permission you can erect the most unbeautiful buildings. And you can make roads wherever you like and as ugly as you like. Then, as a reward you collect marvellous grants from the nonsensical EEC. Pressure groups of farmers and foresters have long had their hearts set on the exploitation of the uplands. In this they are encouraged by sweeping statements from the Countryside Commission, such as: 'Everyone concerned about the uplands can agree on the need to develop the economic life of the uplands'. This is just not true. Everyone does not agree. Take sheep farming, for instance. Some of us fail to see the point of increasing upland sheep production because on such poor land it can never be successful without vast subsidies. In any case we can easily do without the additional produce. Leave the uplands as they are, some of us say, or let them get wilder. As the population grows and the world of microchips and television begins to drive us all mad, we are going to need our wilderness areas more and more.

Effects of a Mild Winter

During a winter in which lizards, snakes and hedgehogs have forgotten to hibernate and hawthorns and larches were green in the middle of January, it is inevitable that strange things are happening among the insects, too. My hive bees, for instance, have been flying every day, going off on long safaris in search of pollen. Moths, too, are abnormally active, some of them months before schedule. One of my favourites, the oak beauty, which I usually begin to see in late March, was out in January. This precocious insect proved to be the first of a procession which included the pale brindled beauty, the March moth, the chestnut, the Hebrew character and the dotted border, all moths that are chancing their luck by coming out so early. But they'll be all right if winter persists so green and mild. Perfect conditions, I am afraid, for a real plague of grey squirrels. An autumn full of acorns and a winter nearly as warm as an average spring have left the squirrels dancing with joy and energy. You don't need to be gifted with foresight to predict plenty of damage to young trees in the coming months. And by late summer I suppose people will be writing to me as they did when squirrels were so abundant a few years ago. Then for two or three weeks I got letters from all over Wales reporting grey squirrels seen high on mountain ridges far from trees.

Mixed Fortunes of Welsh Castles

After the Civil War the Cromwellians were most uneven in their treatment of Welsh castles. Maybe it depended how much hatred a castle had engendered or which side it had been on. Whatever the reasons some castles were severely ruined and others dealt with quite lightly. No doubt the quality of the masonry was also a factor. The mortar used to build by far the biggest castle in Wales, the one at Caerphilly, must have been good stuff, for gunpowder largely failed against it. At most places, once the Cromwellians had done their worst, the castle stones were gradually used to provide materials for modern buildings. So were the old town walls. Tenby, however, is unique in losing practically all its castle but retaining its town walls almost entire. At only two places both castle and town walls survive in great splendour: Conwy and Caernarfon. Conwy's are the more perfect, the best in Britain in fact. Nowhere can you get more vividly the feel of a medieval town. 'It is like an illumination from the chronicles of Froissart', said one commentator. But Caernarfon castle is, I think, more of a spectacle, especially from Menai Strait with all the heights of Snowdonia as background. An intriguing mystery is why the order for the demolition of this castle was never carried out. I wonder if there were already castle enthusiasts in the seventeenth century and if one of them 'forgot' to deliver the message?

The Oldest Town in Wales

South-west from Caernarfon the peninsula of Llŷn stretches out a rugged and muscular arm thirty miles into the Irish Sea, a narrowing arm that begins in the east with the triple sharp peaks of Yr Eifl and after many undulations ends in the west at Bardsey Island. Because it is so accessible from the sea this long peninsula has been freely invaded and colonised since Megalithic times. But Stone Age dolmens and Bronze Age cairns are widely spread in Wales and it is Iron Age Llŷn that really is worth seeing, especially the hill fort of Tre'r Ceiri which caps one of the summits of Yr Eifl at 1,591 feet. You can reach it from the road that climbs south-west from Llanaelhaearn (12 miles south-west of Caernarfon). In about a mile a footpath goes straight up the hillside along a wall, then curves away on a bold zigzag up through sparse heather, lifting you quite gently up to what at first seems a chaos of loose rocks at the top. But as you pick your way through these scattered stones you realise that you are passing through what must once have been considerable walled defences. You will be reminded of Carn Goch in Carmarthenshire if you know that great hill fort. But this place eclipses Carn Goch, not by the extent of the defences but for what you find within them—the copious foundations of a complete town of the Iron Age.

The Call of the Hill Forts

As a Christmas present, kind friends gave me the Ordnance Survey map of Southern Britain in the Iron Age. But to call this just a map is quite misleading. It is also a rich store of information presented in the form of a text of fifty-five pages. So by the time you have digested all this material you are pretty well an expert on the Iron Age before you have even opened the sumptuous map itself which is enormously revealing on the distribution of Iron Age peoples—their earthworks, villages, shrines, dykes, trackways, burials and especially their coinage whose importance the map rightly stresses. It is most striking that in the Iron Age, even more than now, south-east England had got the money and the rest of us had not. The map of Wales, for instance, shows an almost total lack of any coin finds. But what Wales had got, along with south-west England, was an abundance of hill forts which are, I think, far better than all the coins that ever were. For coins have to be sought in museums. But the forts are much as they were two thousand years ago, still crowning the tops of two hundred Welsh hills and headlands. They are places to walk up to and see across to far horizons, to hear the songs of many skylarks and feel the wind in your hair. The noblest gold coin is dross in comparison.

Save our Sand-dunes

The recent gales and floods that have done such damage to houses, promenades, roads and railways on the Welsh coast have left their mark also on sand-dunes. But this is fair enough. Dunes are, after all, the product of storms and down the ages must have been built up and knocked down repeatedly. I don't suppose that in all history many people have tried to live in sand-dunes. But they have settled next door to them. And eventually regretted it when they found the sand blowing about their ears and into their eyes, finally driving them away and burying their dwellings and cultivations. But what the wind brings the wind can take away. A mountain of sand can vanish in one day's hurricane and then behold, the living floors of prehistoric man, his hearths, his tools, his ornaments, lie exposed. But not only ancient man suffered. Records show that in the late Middle Ages and in Tudor times the dunes were also on the move, rolling across farming land and burying villages. Those lands still lie buried. Because sand-dunes are so hostile to human life they have remained wilder than nearly everywhere else. And being so beautiful, fragrant, flowery and natural they all deserve protection from disturbance and exploitation. A few are already National Nature Reserves. But all of them ought to be. For along our long coastline sand-dunes are not so common that we can afford to lose any.

A Famous Path up Snowdon, 1990

Sometime soon I think I must climb Snowdon from the south; it is many years since I tried it that way. This route takes you up that very steep trail known as the Watkin Path, a name that may well remind us of the Channel Tunnel because it was named after Sir Edward Watkin, a railway magnate who last century went to Dover and made a start on the tunnel. But the press whipped up such a furore on grounds of security that the government was forced to stop the scheme. That was in 1883. Six years late Sir Edward may have spotted the following quaint advertisement of the sale of the south side of Snowdon: 'Consider the enjoyment you will be able to give to thousands, the fishing, the climbing, and the joy of allowing people freely to ramble. There are few opportunities ever afforded a man to possess a park like this and know that the people are all able to enjoy it without paying a farthing for it'. Sir Edward Watkin duly bought this romantic piece of Welsh scenery, and seems to have taken to heart what the sales blurb had said: it was not long before he made his now famous path to the summit. So the Snowdonia National Park was being born nearly sixty years before it was at last declared in 1951. I hope that two years from now, on the centenary of the Watkin Path—13 September 1992—the Ramblers Association or someone will honour the memory of Sir Edward, and that of prime minister Gladstone who, aged 83, declared the path open and, standing on a high rock, made a rousing speech on the subject of justice for Wales.

A Railway above the Sea

The wind off the sea was a mere zephyr, the water was calm and the approaching rain had not yet arrived as I made my stumbling way along the rocky shore that lies under the cliffs south of Fairbourne. Botanically I made a good start: a patch of brilliant green on the cliff face turned out, as I got nearer, to be a clump of that beautiful winter-green fern, the sea spleenwort, which is a good find anywhere along this coast. Another treat was the fulmars. Here they were, scores of them in the middle of winter, gliding and circling in courtship display as if it was the height of the breeding season. And those that were not on the wing sat on what will be their nests, and looked calmly down at me from only a few yards above my head. These cliffs are very tall and in places are crumbling dangerously. Yet incredibly the Cambrian Coast railway line finds its way gingerly along them, a feat that is possible only because the fragile crags are constantly being shored up by some stalwart engineering. Massive walls have been built up from the beach, cracks in the rocks have been filled with stone-work and cement, and there is even a shelter built over the line against avalanches. So this walk along the shore is quite as much for railway buffs as for bird-watchers. As I got back to my car the rain arrived and the wind blew suddenly cold. But with my mind full of evergreen ferns and flirtatious fulmars, I felt I had escaped the winter, if only for a couple of hours.

The Great Snows of 1947

Last week the weather was a great topic of conversation, producing all the usual comparisons with previous hard winters. Then the official weatherman declared it the coldest February since 1947. But when I came to compare this 1986 February with my memories of that of 1947 I could not find much resemblance. 1947 was the year of the great snow. Through late January it fell in majestic quantities and drifted day after day so that when February arrived many an upland valley which lay across the wind was already filled to great depth. My wife and I were then living high on the Welsh moors and there were days when we wondered if our little cottage was going to be completely buried in the drifts. Again and again during February the blizzards came back and there was no let-up in the weather until nearly the middle of March. In the deepest hollows the snow packed down and turned into solid ice under its own weight. And there it lay for months, the last to go being in a deep gully high in Snowdonia where the ice did not finally melt until the end of July. The weather forecasts of those days were nowhere near as accurate as those of today and the blizzrds of 1947 arrived with little warning, catching the shepherds off their guard. The sheep had not been brought down off the mountains and they died in huge numbers, sometimes scores of them piled in one heap where they had huddled behind walls for shelter. In retrospect I am glad to have lived through those historic snowfalls. But it was a once-in-a-lifetime experience I have no wish to repeat.

Rivers have Ancient Names

Our local river, the Dyfi, is a stream of great beauty and interest. Having a wild little temper it has managed to keep most human settlements at a distance and so has kept itself sweet-smelling and unpolluted for all its thirty miles. Often fishermen from the town come and spend a whole day alone on its banks and having caught nothing go home contented and refreshed. What further proof is needed of the close links that must have existed between primitive man and rivers? And since for thousands of years the life of early man was intimately bound up with rivers, it is not surprising that we have carefully preserved some of their names from the remotest times of which we have any word-memories.

So even in districts of England where nearly all place names are of German, Norman or Danish origin, the prehistoric names of some rivers survive (Avon, Dove, Exe and so on). In Wales, as in the other remaining fragments of Celtic Europe, all the ancient names are still preserved and are in everyday use. Not only river names such as Hafren (Severn), Gwy (Wye), Dyfrdwy (Dee) and Wysg (Usk), but countless numbers of other place-names which probably date back into pre-Roman times nearly as far as the river-names themselves, their preservation having been assured by that astonishing phenomenon, the long duration and continuing lively survival of the Welsh language.

Old-Style Field Frolics

Because I like to think of people of years ago enjoying the countryside, I treasure accounts of days in the field such as you can occasionally find in the files of old newspapers. A snippet I came upon the other day described an excursion of a society called the Oswestry and Welshpool Naturalists' Field Club. They met at Rhyd-y-mwyn near Mold on Monday, 29 August, 1898 and walked up the Alun Valley to the Loggerheads where they had tea before a carriage came and took them back to their starting place. How genteel of them to meet on a Monday! Of course there were at least two clergymen in the party because that was still the age when rural parsons had leisure and were prominent among the country's naturalists. The occasion was a botanical one and their finds included lime-loving plants like frog orchid, marjoram, rock stonecrop, ploughman's spikenard, lesser meadow-rue, saw-wort, field gentian as well as the plant we so vulgarly call 'bloody cranesbill' but which they noted down as 'crimson geranium'. Those were the days of small, very local natural history groups. On the same page of the newspaper I see that another party, this time it was the Offa Field Club, met on a Thursday at Llansanffraid. They also botanised on the limestone, visited a hill fort and an interesting old church, and got back at nine in the evening, by carriage of course. Happy days!

Cormorant in the Storm

On Tuesday morning a tremendous wind and a spring tide came up the estuary together. When I went out an hour before the official time of high tide I found the sea already pouring over the sea-wall and soon it was flowing deeply across the fields. For three hours or more the flood continued to spread until there was nothing to see but miles of water between us and the eastward hills. Frequent squalls lashed the flood with heavy rain, turning the water from black to white as they passed. When the water rose in the fields countless small creatures were floated up out of earth and grass to lie struggling helplessly on the surface. Immediately a host of black-headed gulls and common gulls came to flutter over the water, picking up the easy food with graceful swoops to the surface. Hurricane gusts and blinding rain which obviously meant nothing to them sent me scurrying to take shelter in the lee of the boat-house. But I was not the first arrival. For there standing on one leg, his head plunged deep into his back feathers, was a cormorant. In the boom and thunder of the gale he did not hear me arrive, nor noticed me as I crouched beside him. Even when I lightly stroked his neck he did not wake up, so profound was the sleep of this presumably gale-wearied fowl. So man and bird took shelter till the squalls had passed.

Walking the Line to Barmouth

If you come walking in Snowdonia the chances are that you will make straight for the mountains. But perhaps there will be one day during your stay when the summits will have retreated into the clouds or you won't feel quite up to tackling those 3,000-footers. This will be your cue to take to the Barmouth Estuary trail, which is perfectly level all the way because it keeps to the old railway track from Dolgellau to the sea. After five miles of this lovely walk, you come to the coast near Fairbourne. But you mustn't give up then because, if you do, you miss the *pièce de résistance* of the whole walk: the footpath along the famous viaduct to Barmouth. You don't need to be a railway enthusiast to appreciate this bridge. Besides having an honoured place in railway history, it also has splendid prospects of this incomparable estuary. Then if, having crossed the bridge, you still have plenty of puff and are a bit bored with so many horizontal miles, you can go along the road towards the town and very soon turn to the right and climb more than a hundred steep steps up into a glorious wilderness of rocks and bracken owned by the National Trust. From there, you will look back over the estuary to one of the really great prospects of Wales. It is especially good in winter when, as I saw it one afternoon this week, the sun is going down into the sea and doing wonderful things with the light on Cader Idris, turning its snowfields into a kaleidoscope of pinks, blues and purples.

A Precocious Saxifrage

Everybody has their story of how the recent mild weather affected nature, but the most original to come my way is from a *Guardian* reader near Lincoln who wrote on 29 January that he had lately gathered and eaten wild mushrooms and had found perfect specimens of other fungi, including field blewits, wood blewits and the oyster mushroom. His letter inspired me to take to the hills on Wednesday to inspect an old friend among the alpine plants, the purple saxifrage, which is known for its early responses to mild winters. I set off rejoicing that after two days of gales, the wind had fallen light. But I had not gone far up Cader Idris before I found that the wind and the rain were still raging wildly there. Two ravens croaking overhead were a welcome sight for I have always seen the raven as a bird of good omen. And, sure enough, as I came near the cliffs the wind and the rain died away completely. As I struggled up the slippery wet scree to the crags where the saxifrage grows, I was resigned to the probability that the whole alpine vegetation would still be in its winter dormancy. But for once the mountain gods were smiling. Unbelievably the very first plant I looked at offered me a fully open purple flower of this most astonishing of all our saxifrages. My mission accomplished, I decided to test the forbearance of the gods no further on these hazardous rocks. It was enough that I had seen even one flower as early as 3 February, something I'm sure will never happen to me again.

Stoat Gymnastics

Recently I mentioned a pair of stoats that were visiting our bird-table. Since then we have seen them regularly and have been able to learn something about their food preferences. By long tradition stoats are invariably portrayed as bloodthirsty. But, from what I have seen lately, I would say that they will sample pretty well everything, and are very happy to settle for meat and two vegetables at lunch-time, which is when they always appear at our bird-table. Yesterday there was a very strange episode. One of the stoats appeared to go quite berserk, dashing all over the lawn at a tremendous rate in a series of wild zigzags. Then he executed a succession of forward gambols at the same breakneck speed. Things got even wilder when he leapt high into the air several times, landing flat on his back but immediately raced on again. I soon realised that I was witnessing the famous dancing of the stoat, a stunt by which rabbits and birds are supposed to be so fascinated that they venture very close out of curiosity. The crafty stoat, so the tale goes, then suddenly leaps out and seizes the victim from among the circle of bewitched spectators. I have always put this story firmly amongst those about shaggy dogs and now that I have seen the act for myself I am even more sceptical. For no rabbits or birds arrived as witnesses and I would have sworn that the stoat, far from playing a clever part, was in reality having some sort of a fit. So I prefer to believe that stoats suffer from a strange nervous disorder that causes these outlandish performances.

MARCH

A Man who loved Nasty Birds

In these parts, as I recall with pleasure, we used to have a character with an unorthodox attitude to nature. Being a wealthy landowner he could afford to indulge his particular eccentricity, which was bird-protection of a very special kind. We all know that our legislators have decided for us which birds are nice and which are nasty, some indeed so nasty that not even bird-protection societies will usually raise a finger in their defence. It was this second group, the out-and-out vermin, that our eccentric landowner chose to protect.

All the detested crow tribe found sanctuary in his woods (and what he said to the pests officer who came to reduce the rookery may not be printable but it was effective). And sparrowhawks and woodpigeons nested peacefully in his coverts, along with a whole eisteddfod of rabbits, badgers, polecats, foxes, stoats and weasels.

Which was satisfactory so far as it went. But the fate of one bird worried him: the cormorant, then so persecuted by angling interests. For cormorants, being waterbirds, naturally never sought the shelter of his waterless estate. There was only one thing to do: to acquire the rights of a stretch of cliff complete with nesting cormorants and make it a bird sanctuary. Which, after long negotiations, he succeeded in doing. Now, some years after his death, his cragful of cormorants still thrives, a lasting monument, be it hoped, to a friend of birds that are not quite nice.

Parish Archives

Our parish is a network of old roads that served now abandoned farms, houses, quarries, mines and peat-cuttings. And there are some whose purpose is obscure, climbing gently across naked hillsides but leading nowhere. My guess is that they were access roads to forests we have lost; for at one time this rather bare-looking parish must have been exceptionally well-wooded, our most distinguished ancient monument being a charcoal-consuming furnace.

Disused roads, like ruined houses, disappear quicker than you might think possible. Like one that climbs up out of our valley to the mooland and is now such a faint and shadowy mark in the turf that I thought it must have been abandoned back in the Middle Ages, until a shepherd who lives near it told me he remembered it in use and with its drains opened annually up to fifty years ago.

Roads can be awful mischief-makers, involving quarrels over rights of way, maintenance and modernisation. They wind in and out of our parish records, causing trouble at every turn. I like our parish council's firm rebuff in 1910 to the would-be modernisers of one of our bridges (I leave the spelling as I find it): 'It was unanimously decided that we consider a footbridge 3ft. wide is quite sufficient to meet the traffic in an unpopulace district and over a small brook where there is no Vehicle (car) hardly never passing.'

Could You Make a Cart-Wheel? (1959)

Few men these days can make a pair of cart-wheels, a pair so exactly alike that they would run sweetly together and continue to do so year after year. The perfection of such wheels results from the judgment inherited by craftsmen down the generations. And now the craft dies fast, for a young wheel-wright is a rarity in the countryside, especially one who can tyre a wheel as well as make one. The tractor-driving farm-hands of the future will not even know what timbers are needed for a wheel: ash for preference for the felloes, oak, nothing but oak, for the spokes, elm for the hub. Perhaps the very word felloe is doomed to disappear or become a mere book-word. If so, people will soon forget that it was usually pronounced 'felly'.

I suppose the most striking difference between the products of individual craftsmanship and those of mass-production is in the length of time they endure. Motor vehicles are not intended to last many years. Farm-carts may last for generations. Recently, a farmer near here took a cart-wheel to be respoked by a local wheel-wright. The wheel-maker recognised the wheel as his own work and on separating the felloes was able to point to his initials in the joint and the date 1904. Which demonstrates both the age of our wheel-wright and the quality of his work.

A Fox on Gower's Cliffs

One day last week I found myself on those limestone cliffs of south Wales whose caves are reckoned to have been the haunts of our very earliest forbears. Regretting not having come at low tide when the caves are accessible, I fell to examining the near-by inland cliffs. And there a hundred and fifty feet above me I espied an opening. Suppose this were an unexplored cave, I thought. What might I not find in it? But I had to climb up there first. The first hundred feet were simple. Then a harder twenty-five up to a ledge. But the final twenty-five feet, demanding a risky squirm round a bulge, defeated me. Then, as I stared up at the entrance, I got a surprise that nearly unbalanced me off my ledge. A face slowly appeared round a rock and eyes looked down into mine. A few dream-like seconds passed before this half-shadowed face resolved itself into that of a fox. I waited to see what he would do next. Surely he would slink back into the cave? Nothing of the sort. He was coming out and was prepared to wait till I had shifted. We stared unblinkingly at each other for several minutes. Then I surrendered and scrambled down from the ledge. Whereupon the fox nonchalantly leapt to where I had been sitting and raced beautifully away up the face and was gone in a few seconds.

'A Dog Idealised'

Often in the past few weeks we have heard a fox barking at night in the wood near our house and one morning two were seen playing together outside the wood. When disturbed they ran across the field with that unhurried gait that foxes have and before slipping into the wood both of them paused and looked back over their shoulders. Then even our fox-detesting farmer-neighbour was moved to utter a few admiring comments. For they looked extremely good, the two of them standing there so richly red and so vividly alive in the morning sun. W. H. Hudson relates how when he once got a close view of an early morning fox he was struck by the superiority of the appearance of the wild fox over the domestic dog. For him at that moment the fox seemed 'a dog idealised and made beautiful.'

No wonder the fox is so popular as an animal of the chase. For the animals most hunted for sport are commonly the most beautiful and graceful, such as deer and hares and foxes, as if to kill what is especially beautiful adds a spice to killing. In the wilder parts of Wales there is little tradition of fox-hunting as a sport. Here the fox has always been treated as vermin. Yet despite a long and determined persecution the fox proves ever resilient. Thousands are annually destroyed. Yet their number grows not less. It is as if each year they spring by spontaneous regeneration from the mountain rocks.

Welsh Castles, Welsh Language (1962)

The other day I was at Castell y Bere, the medieval castle between Cader Idris and the sea. How changed, how face-lifted it is compared with what it was a few years ago. It used to crouch concealed upon its mound, a mysterious ruin quite buried in trees and undergrowth. But now it has had the full Ministry of Works treatment. The site has been laid bare, the old walls have received a most generous application of cement and now they stand conspicuously white and scrubbed-looking above the valley. One can only hope that this antiseptic look is but temporary and that lichens, moss and ferns will be allowed to tone it down. At the moment you might be forgiven if, from a distance, you mistook the site for the beginning of a new power station.

The trouble we go to in order to preserve our ancient monuments! Yet the oldest and most remarkable man-made thing in Wales is commonly scorned even by some Welsh people. I mean the Welsh language, a tongue so ancient as to make the oldest of the so-called ancient monuments seem like something reported in yesterday's paper. Just because a language is not something you can see and touch and plaster with cement and put an officious little fence round and charge sixpence admission for, it is allowed to rust and rot away while we go to enormous expense to shore up the castles of medieval tyrants.

Across the Pages of History

Go in any direction from this little town of Machynlleth and you can soon be up in the loneliness of the hills. So, in Tuesday's warm sunshine, I went northwards up a valley that was at first dark with spruces. But in a mile I came up into a wild and sunlit world of grassy slopes climbing to distant uplands. I passed beneath a fine old oakwood which, higher up, gave place to a scatter of hawthorns. Then there were no more trees, only endless grasslands grazed by the quiet sheep of the hills. This is a silent and beautiful place but was not always so. The nineteenth century made a violent intrusion here. Slate was mined deep into the hillsides and great tips of rock waste were vomited down the slopes. Then the industry died, the mining community disappeared and now all that is left are the great barren spoil heaps and many roofless sheds whose walls are green with ferns. When in some future century the archaeologists dig here they will be amazed at the extent of the lost civilisation that once flourished in this remote spot. Two miles further into the hills the valley ends and your only escape is up formidable slopes. Even here, near the alpine zone, lead-miners were busy long ago but now their traces are getting faint. And that is how it is all over the uplands. You will not go far without coming upon old mines, deserted quarries, abandoned shepherds' houses or far more ancient and mysterious walls now half-buried in the turf. In fact, walking the hills is like walking across the pages of history.

A Rare Little Fern Survives

A botanical game I like to play is dropping in on old friends among the plants—and the longer the gap since you last saw them, the greater the pleasure in finding them still safe and well. But it does not always work out like that: sometimes you find them sickly or diminished, sometimes completely vanished. So it was with trepidation that I set off up a side-stream of the river Dyfi to check up on a rare little fern called the forked spleenwort, which some friends and I found many years ago and had not visited since. I was not sure that I would remember the spot exactly—all I could recall was that it grew on a small rock face, high up a hillside and above a small block of conifers. At botanist's speed, which is no speed at all, I toiled up a brackeny slope, then up a murderous scree, until I was looking down on the little conifer patch. But what I had remembered as a single rock face turned out to be a series of crags stretching across the slope for over a mile. Never mind, it is the quest that matters, I reminded myself. The search ended much sooner than I had dared to hope. Neither time nor acid rain had harmed that little fern in the slightest. Certainly it was withered and brown, for that is its winter condition. Otherwise it was exactly as I remembered it—just a few sparse fronds, the only shred of vegetation on an outcrop of hard, dry rock. I never cease to marvel at the persistence of rare species always poised on the edge of extinction.

Encounter with a Friendly Adder

Pushing my way through a reed-bed I reached a little clearing and stopped abruptly. On a slight mound about six paces ahead lay three adders coiled up side by side sunbathing. Outside in the fields a cold wind blew. But here in the reeds the adders had their private suntrap. And I had by chance burst in on it, my heavy gum-boots sending tremors for several yards through the quaking ground. But adders in the spring are notoriously torpid and these three were so unmoved by my intrusion that I could observe them as long as I liked. Two were males, beautifully silver and black. Between them lay a quite different female for she was reddish-brown. I inched my way forward to see how near I could get. At three yards one of the males raised his head, flickered his tongue and slid silently into the reeds. At two yards the other male did the same. But the female, perhaps more hibernation-sleepy or sun-intoxicated, was much more oblivious of danger. She lay in a rigid coil, her narrow little head poised high and unmoving. When I softly stroked the top of her head she was totally indifferent. And it was not until I stroked her back right down to the tip of her tail that she decided it was time to go. Strange creatures, snakes.

Leeks or Daffodils?

By St David's Day, thanks to the mildest of winters, all wild daffodils will be in bloom. Which is appropriate enough for a flower that is the national emblem of Wales. Or is it? What, you may well ask, what about the poor old leek? As an old Welsh emblem the leek is fully authenticated. Shakespeare could not have risked a whole scene about a Welshman and a leek unless his audience already knew all about Welshmen and leeks. So the connections must go back well beyond Shakespeare. Possibly right to the ancient Celtic world. I would bet the Breton, Cornish, Welsh and Irish languages shared pretty well the same word for leek before the Romans came. So with all this antiquity behind their old emblem why should the Welsh be changing to daffodils? It is, I fear, all a bit snobbish, this preference for the sweetly odorous daffodil. Perhaps it is all Wordsworth's fault. And those who have pushed the daffodil forward are lucky in having a linguistic coincidence to help it on its way. For the Welsh for daffodil (*cenhinen Pedr*) happens to be the same as the Welsh for leek (*cenhinen*) provided you invoke St Peter. A daffodil, translated from Welsh, is 'St Peter's leek'. So with the church to bless it what could be more respectable? So I am afraid in the long run the daffodil must prevail. After all, a chap does look rather ridiculous with a leek in his buttonhole, doesn't he?

Easter on Snowdon

Easter Sunday was a lovely day for climbing Snowdon and all the world and his wife were there, along with lots of their children and no shortage of grandparents. Some were loaded with immense rucksacks containing I can't imagine what. Others were not carrying so much as a paper bag. Some wore strong mountain boots and carried ice axes and crampons. Others, to the consternation of the National Park wardens, were in plimsolls as if it were midsummer's day. It is always a problem to know what to wear on mountains. Normally you start in the warmth of the valley and are tempted to go lightly clad and then you freeze on the summit. But Sunday was the opposite. A chill wind blew across the carpark and most people put on all their woollies. Yet what happened? By the time they reached the snow at about 2,000 feet they were peeling off their anoraks and sweaters in the sun. But everyone was happy. For most it was the first breath of fresh air they'd had for months and there was a general holiday atmosphere. I couldn't help contrasting this with what people were writing about mountains two centuries ago. Thomas Pennant, describing a corrie in Snowdonia, said it was 'environed with horrible precipices, a fit place to inspire murderous thoughts'. Since then the mountains haven't changed but people have. Pennant could not have written that today. I suspect it was really the solitude that got him down and that if he had been on Snowdon this Easter he would have been as cheerful as everybody else.

The Migrant Swans of March, 1984

This week the wild swans came. I saw them far away in the early dusk, a pure white line across the mud of the darkening estuary. Here, every year without fail, in the first days of March, these Bewick's swans from Ireland come dropping in like old friends. But only for a couple of hours or so. They have spring in their blood and they know that the ice is about to melt on their breeding grounds in Russia. As we live in an age of bird-counts I felt obliged to put a figure on my swans. Very slowly I walked towards them across the saltmarsh until the white streak began to break up into individual birds. Now I could hear their voices. They were chatting privately among themselves, a continuous gentle conversation that filled the twilight with musical croonings and honkings. How long they have been making this annual spring journey we shall never know. But what is certain is that we live in drainage-mad days, that huge wetlands have been reclaimed in the last two centuries and that for swans the world is still rapidly shrinking. There is a very long tradition of man's dislike of the wilderness. And not so long ago a distinguished historian described the reclamation of marshes as 'beneficial to everyone'. Such blinkered attitudes are still widespread. For even in these days when millions are entranced by nature programmes on television, very few people really know, care or understand about the needs of swans and other creatures of the wild.

A Wildflower of Poor Repute

A plant now green in woods and hedge-bottoms is dog's mercury. I suppose the dog's part of the name is contemptuous, implying that our ancestors regarded it as a worthless plant in contrast with its cousin the annual mercury which was a valued herb. Dog's mercury is abundant in many British counties. But in this part of Wales it is just scarce enough to give us joy when we find it. For it tells us that the soil there is good, not only fertile but moist and cool, the sort of ground worth searching for other, choicer plants like early purple orchid or maybe even herb paris which likes to hide itself in patches of dog's mercury. I admit that this mercury isn't much to look at. It lacks petals, offends the nose and is said to be poisonous. But it brings an end to winter as surely as primroses and celandines. Not that everyone loves it. Some gardeners for instance go in dread of it. Witness Reginald Farrer of Yorkshire who said: 'Of all weeds there is none more odious and pernicious and dislikable in every way'. Strong words when you think of all the other terrifying invaders, from couch grass to convolvulus, on which he could have poured his words of hate. But as it does not trouble us here in our sour-soiled garden I am sure we shall go on admiring this mercury that is fit only for dogs.

A Mild Winter Brings Floods

As I write this the rain is lashing at our windows, the wind roars in the oaks above the house and the high tide is surging up the estuary and pouring over the sea defences. East and west there is a glint of floods near and far and our solitary old house in the marshes is cut off by deepish water. In these conditions moles and other creatures of the soil must be in great distress and only ducks are happy. Though this is a district notorious for floods, not even the oldest inhabitants can recall such long weeks of rough weather off the Atlantic nor a time when the river has so often been over its banks. Yet even without the dramatic weather I would have called this week remarkable. In fact, before the latest storm broke on Monday night I had decided to devote this diary to what had until then been on everybody's lips, the phenomenally early blossoming of the gardens. I felt like Gilbert White who in 1781 wrote: 'My garden is in nice order and full of flowers. Lilies, roses, fraxinellas, red valerians and irises now make a gaudy show'. But he was writing in June whereas we could make a similar claim right now. It is really quite ridiculous to see some of our camellias, rhododendrons and magnolias flowering weeks before their time. We know they will probably be blasted by the frosts; but meanwhile we enjoy a sight and a fragrance we will almost certainly never experience again so early in the year, unless of course the greenhouse effect really is operating already.

Barn Owl Neighbours

This old house where we have been living for nearly thirty years used to be a farmhouse. These days the cattle have long since gone from the buildings and now we have much more agreeable neighbours, a pair of barn owls. Until they first nested here two years ago these beautiful white owls had always seemed as remote as dreams as they hunted over the marshes in the twilight. But now we know a little more about them. Their almost complete silence, for example. In fact, it was several weeks before we were sure whether they had a nest or not. Then one day I went into the building and could faintly hear the twittering voices of young ones high above my head. How different from the tawny owls which hoot so loudly and persistently and whose young ones just now are shrieking for food all night in the trees round the house. The great moment last time the barn owls nested here was when their young could first fly. For several evenings in early July we saw four of them and their parents fluttering about in the dusk and the garden seemed full of white wings. A crucial thing about our barn owls here is that they breed in a nest-box. Otherwise the farm building is quite without suitable breeding ledges. Throughout the countryside there must be countless old buildings where barn owls would live happily if nest-boxes were provided. I am sure nothing would do more to stop the decline of these very desirable birds. All they want is a big box in a dark place.

Salute to the RSPB, 1989

This week I am in reminiscent mood because it is just thirty years since my wife and I came to live in this grey old farmhouse between the woods and the estuary. In those days this beautiful estate belonged to a shy, retiring man who kept it as a private nature reserve. When he died his widow sold the property, on very fair terms, to the Royal Society for the Protection of Birds. Since then pools have been created, hundreds of nest-boxes provided and a multitude of trees planted. But the greatest change is that now people come here in far greater numbers than formerly. Yet this has in no way reduced the value of the place as a refuge for nature. Those who come here are sympathetic to the cause. They behave well. They find their way to the hides along carefully planned trails, and the disturbance is minimal. That they come to beautiful reserves like this is enormously important. In a world that worships economic growth, which means ever more urbanisation, motorways, airports and factories, what chance is there that anything green will be left a hundred years from now? Maybe the only hope is a rapid increase in public concern about the ecological health of the earth. And what better way of acquiring such concern than by visiting a well-managed wildlife reserve, and learning to appreciate high-quality countryside? This year the RSPB celebrates their centenary. I pray that when their bi-centenary comes round they will be able to look back at many more wild places they have been able to save from the grasping hands of exploiters, both public and private.

All that Glitters

One day I was in the Golden Valley in Herefordshire and it was raining. The woods were leafless, black and wet. Fields were sodden. Streams were overbrimming. Dark hills rose all round and disappeared into darker clouds. I stood under a holly hedge sheltering not from the rain, for that was inescapable, but from the gusting south-west wind. As the water trickled down my neck I wondered how such a place ever came to be called 'golden'. The beaches of Tahiti I could believe are truly golden: but except for a fortnight in late summer when the corn is ripe, could this dark dripping valley under the Black Mountains ever be golden?

I looked at the River Dore coming down full and fleet from upland Wales. I began to speculate about the name of this stream. Because, I said to myself, nearly all the streams along this border—Lugg, Teme, Arrow, Severn and the rest—have names of Welsh origin, presumably Dore has come from the Welsh *dŵr,* meaning water. Maybe our Norman masters back in the eleventh century, indifferent to the niceties of philology, heard the word '*dŵr*' but wrote it as 'd'or' and the valley has glittered with false gold ever since? So from floundering through waterlogged fields I blundered into the bogs of place-name etymology. Is there any more dangerous ground for the untutored than that?

APRIL

Shelducks get Matey

Now it is shelduck time. I mean that now, if you care to, you can go and sit quietly in the woods at dawn and soon you will see these large and colourful ducks come flying across from the estuary, whistling and quacking as they come. And if you are well hidden they will come fluttering ever so lightly down through the branches and land among the anemones and primroses on the woodland floor. Now you will observe their courtship ceremonial. And if this is nothing nearly so elaborate and animated as that of blackcock or ruff, it is still quite something to witness. For if they simply stood and did nothing they would be worth watching, so strange is it to see these essentially mud-flat fowl suddenly opting for the sylvan life. I would say they enjoy the change. They seem so happy standing or walking rather solemnly about in the green shadows of the trees, occasionally showing a bit of feeling by running after each other with heads bowed to the ground. Or else they wander meditatively away up the wood to choose a nesting burrow. But perhaps I am cruel to suggest that to see them you must go to the draughty dawn woods in this cold east wind. So let me assure you that there is an afternoon performance also, when it is much more agreeable to sit around in woods. That is the one I invariably go to.

Birth of a Moorland Stream, 1960

You can have a fine walk over the Cardigan moors to the source of the Tywi river, a wide shallow saucer of gently sloping bogland. The river rises from many springs round the edge of this saucer and flows in many streams and runnels to the centre through bog-moss, sparse heather, white tussocks of moor-grass and patches of red rushes. One day there a fox rose from a heather couch, ran for two hundred yards, stopped and looked back at me, ran another two hundred yards, stopped and looked back again; and so on till he was gone from sight far across the hills.

This is quite empty country. Not a house, not even a ruin in sight, a place given over to sheep, ravens, buzzards and singing larks. At the southern edge of this peaty basin the tiny river slips silently out through a gap in the grey rocks. Here it is almost lost among the rushes. But in half a mile it is three yards wide and wriggling in its valley; and its wine-red waters are noisy on a pebbly bed. In another half-mile it goes down its first waterfall which drops no more than a yard, then plunges into its first gorge whose sides are not six feet high. Thus early in life does the Tywi assert its personality. For all down its length it will swing from side to side and cut gorges and make waterfalls wherever it can. In so doing it creates some of the really great scenery of Wales.

A Motte Worth Having

A useful thing to have around is a motte and bailey. Or rather a motte is. And in case you would not recognise one if you saw one, perhaps I had better describe the one nearest here. It stands on the river bank in a commanding position. It is a steep-sided, flat-topped hillock and must have been well built to have kept its shape so well since early Norman times. It was probably not built by the Normans but raised in imitation of them by some Welsh chieftain anxious to impress his neighbours that he was worthy of the dignity and privileges of a manorial lord. In later Norman times you were nobody unless you had a castle of stone; but in the early days after 1066 a simple mound (or motte) with a wooden palisade was good enough.

The bailey defences of our local mound have rotted away long since and been replaced by what is infinitely preferable, a group of trees. But the motte still commands the river and hence its usefulness. You can creep up its flank and get an excellent view of the ducks and waders that frequent that part of the river. Besides, the pines that crown it house a heronry and a raven's nest; and shelducks hatch their eggs in holes in its sides. So it probably serves a better purpose now than at any time in its history.

Golden Glory

Gorse, the prickly gorse of wayside and common, beloved by stonechats, despised by farmers, detested by bare-footed picknickers, is a plant of past glory. But I did not realise just how glorious was its past until lately when a kind friend sent me what I fancy is a little-known book published in 1960 by the National Museum of Ireland. In this fascinating survey we are given 200 pages on the past importance of gorse in Ireland. But many of its uses were undoubtedly widespread elsewhere.

To compile this book, which is called simply, *Furze* (you do not speak of gorse in Ireland) the author, A.T. Lucas, went back to Edward Lhuyd's method when he inquired into the Celtic world two hundred and fifty years ago—the questionnaire. Inquiry-forms about gorse were sent to all parts of Ireland and this book summarises the answers received. From them it appears that gorse was used for at least a thousand years as cattle-fodder, baker's oven-fuel, road-foundations, field-drains and other fascinating uses and was cultivated in rows in fields like any other crop. Now that gorse has practically gone out of use perhaps it is fated to become quite uncommon. In some English counties a good spread of gorse is already a rarity and will become impossible to find if ever the remaining commons get reclaimed. And when the gorse has gone yet another of the beauties of the British countryside will have departed.

The Way of an Empress

This last week I have been admiring the patience of moths. Since last summer I have had a cocoon in a tin on my bookshelf. Nearly a week ago there emerged from it an emperor moth which I was pleased to find was a female. Now, I thought, I can test this creature's famous power of attracting males. So I placed her on the heather outside the garden to await their arrival. The day was grey and cold and by evening no mate had come. Next day the same story, and the two following. She lay torpid under the cold flow of the east wind. At times the sun shone but not warmly and no male moths arrived.

Yesterday, the fifth day, looked as if it were going to be a repetition of the others. But around midday the wind dropped. At three o'clock the clouds parted and for the first time this year the sun shone really hot on our hillside. At half-past three a male emperor came flickering along the slope straight to the female and mated with her. They were together for an hour, the female completely still, the male occasionally vibrating his wings very slightly. Then he flew away.

The female made not the least movement until dusk. Then, without shifting her position, she laid two or three dozen silvery eggs clustered round a heather stalk. Then she rested the whole night and is still there this morning.

Hare Madness, 1960

Though the woods here are teeming with wild beasts I admit you don't often see them. Not that this is surprising, for very few of them exceed an ounce in weight (dormice, woodmice, voles and shrews) and most are nocturnal. So if you go to the woods by day only, you'd never have reason to suspect the multitudes of very small mammals asleep just under your feet. And with the carnivores of our woods also being mainly night-active, we're not left with much to see by day except squirrels, rabbits and hares, for we have no deer. But red squirrels, even here, are getting scarcer; the newly come grey squirrels are exceedingly furtive; and rabbits are still fairly uncommon.

So for day-time that really only leaves us the hare, the quite unpredictable, altogether delightful hare, and even he snoozes a lot of the daylight away. But not this morning. For as I scribble this, sitting in the wood with my back against an oak, there are four lovely big hares, as red as foxes in the bright sun, chasing wildly through the trees on what is evidently a roughly circular course; for every few minutes they all four come galloping by in Indian file with a reckless disregard of the row they are making on the dead leaves. They take no notice of me at all though they pass within a few yards of me every time. Mad as April hares in fact.

A Community now Vanished

How easy it is to get a wrong idea about a place. There is a tract of country near here I know well, or thought I did; a stretch of peat-bogs and marshes, edged by tangled woods and dotted with little tree-crowned outcrops of slatey rock. A wild, empty, curlew-haunted place that looks as if it has lain unchanged since the world began. I might have gone all my life having no different idea of it than this were it not for the chance remark of an old man of the village. A century or more ago, he said, all round these marshes were scattered cottages of the sort that, being built in one night, could claim squatters' rights.

I then looked at the scene as if for the first time. Gone now were the wild marshes and woods, the primal wilderness. Instead, here was a place where a populous community had lived or rather, I suppose, scratched together some kind of an existence in an unkind world. Presumably they worked when there was work to be had. For the rest they seemed to have existed off the land; and off the near-by estuary too, judging by the layers of cockle-shells still to be unearthed near the sites of their dwellings. Today nothing remains above ground to speak of this forgotten hamlet and its people except a few hollies they planted against the sea winds.

A Halcyon Day

Not often is a kingfisher caught off its guard. So yesterday I was surprised to be able to creep up on one as it dug out a nest-hole in the bank of a stream. My success was pure fluke. I was not even looking for kingfishers but just happened to be standing behind a stream-side alder when I heard one whistling nearby. I looked up-stream and down and was puzzled to see nothing though the calling continued loudly. But eventually I noticed a trickle of sand dropping into the water from a hole in the opposite bank and I realised that a kingfisher was tunnelling there. It had never occurred to me that these birds may shriek even when digging their nests. I now lay on the ground to observe for half an hour, though all I saw most of the time was just a hole in a bank. But every three or four minutes I was rewarded by the most brilliant display of colour I have ever seen on a bird. For at pretty regular intervals the kingfisher came shooting out of the hole, fluttered round for a second practically under my nose and then dived back out of sight. Once inside it continued to shriek. Too excited about everything to be able to keep quiet, I suppose. But isn't it pretty reckless of kingfishers to advertise their nests so blatantly?

Houses Under the Sand

It is an accepted belief that our sand-dunes, especially the oldest ones, are a product of times long ago when, so the theory goes, the weather became much stormier and produced gales which quickly piled up the extensive dunes we know today. The evidence for this in Wales comes from both prehistory and history. In modern times along the Glamorgan coast, when gales have scoured away the sand down to the original soil level, quite a number of prehistoric artefacts have been revealed. There also a medieval settlement is reputed to have been overwhelmed by sand. Similarly at Newborough dunes in Anglesey a tradition has come down of a village of the Middle Ages being abandoned as the sand advanced and smothered it. Such legends are an enjoyable part of our folklore but they take on an extra dimension if someone stumbles on evidence that shows them to be true. This has happened at the now pine-covered Newborough dunes and I was happy this week to join a party of students from Salford University when, under the guidance of the Forestry Commission, we were shown the substantial remains of a cottage recently excavated out of a sand-dune. It was quite moving to see these long-buried walls and to speculate on their age. And also to sense that many more such buildings, each with its story to tell, probably lie beneath the sands all around.

At a Statesman's Grave

At Llanystumdwy last week I stopped to look at its fine old seventeenth-century bridge. Then I walked along the tree-shaded river bank to Lloyd George's grave and found it so sensitively designed it is fitter for a poet then a politician. (Query: should politicians' graves be allowed to clutter up beauty spots?) I remembered the story my father use to tell of a riotous meeting in Birmingham Town Hall in 1900 when Lloyd George, having angered the crowd by speaking against the Boer War, only escaped lynching by slipping out of the back door disguised as a policeman. Meditating that I would have preferred the anti-war Lloyd George of 1900 to the war-hero of 1918, I went on upstream until in a couple of miles I came to a much more interesting grave. This is a splendid dolmen behind the village of Rhos-lan (map reference 483408), its gigantic capstone still lying firmly on the uprights on which it was so cunningly placed some 5,000 years ago. I daresay this too was only a politician's grave but it will probably still be there 5,000 years after Lloyd George is as forgotten as whoever was buried in this dolmen. But life is made up of the things of everyday and when I got back to Llanystumdwy I was delighted to find on display at the local museum the very policeman's helmet in which Lloyd George made his famous escape!

The Vulnerability of Gower

Lately I was in Gower; which is another way of saying that I was in one of the most beautiful and delicate bits of southern Britain. Beautiful because of its limestone cliffs, its wild, green, seaward slopes, its yellow sands, its far views of seas and mountains. Delicate because right across the threshold of this so endearing but so small peninsula is flung a great town. How understandable, if you work in Swansea or Port Talbot, to want to live out in the pure air and total loveliness of Gower. Many have achieved this already. Many more will want to as time goes on. So the bungalow tide creeps ever westwards and the future does not look good. But so far there is much that is almost as virgin, almost as untrampled as it must have been when the megalith builders scattered their copious monuments about the land all those centuries ago. Take Oxwich Bay as an example. Here are wonderful sands (and sea-washed sand can stand all the trampling in the world); behind the sands great reed-beds and fishy channels; then a fine mantle of woodland and a castle ruin peeping through the leaves. All this is set between a long, bare headland in the east and a heavily wooded point in the west. It is so perfect that one says instinctively: long may all speculators, all get-rich-quickers be kept out of such a place.

Companiable Milestones

I wonder, when we have gone completely metric, shall we have kilometre stones along the roads as they have long had all over France? I suppose not. Such stones have had their day. Yet it is strange to think that not only milestones but even standard miles did not come into general use until an act of 1744 required the turnpike trusts to erect stones at intervals of 1,760 yards along roads. Before then milestones were few, for there was a colossal gap in our history, between Roman and modern times, when milestones were almost unknown. But the eighteenth and nineteenth centuries certainly made up for it. I was reminded of this lately when travelling through north Wales along the A5 and seeing Telford's milestones still sentinel at the wayside after 150 years. Some of these have curious place-names on them. Great prominence, for instance, is given in Denbighshire to a place called Cernioge and in Anglesey to somewhere called Mona. But these, when you inquire, are not villages nor towns but merely houses that were used by Telford as changing places for horses. You will still find them on the map: Cernioge is near Pentrefoelas and Mona near Gwalchmai. It would be sad to see all milestones disappear, even though we do not get the pleasure from them that they gave to more leisured travellers. As one of these said in the eighteenth century: 'They enliven a tedious journey and are a peacable company in solitude'. Oh, for solitude on the A5 today!

Owl on a Poet's Gravestone

Owls are birds to some people; but they are omens to others, especially when seen in country graveyards. The other day I called at the church of Llanwnog in Montgomeryshire, a medieval building of special interest because conspicuous in its dark walls you can see blocks of reddish sandstone that were obviously brought there from the defences of Roman Caersws, a mile or so to the south. Inside the church are an ancient rood loft and screen with carvings of foliage and winged dragons. The solid oak steps which formerly led up to the rood loft survive in the thickness of the walls. In the churchyard is the grave of Ceiriog, one of the best-known poets of nineteenth-century Wales. He lived at Caersws and was manager of the narrow-gauge railway which ran from there up to the now extinct lead mines at Van. I was thinking about Ceiriog as I walked from the church porch down the avenue of limes to the gate when, by a fascinating coincidence, a tawny owl flew out of the trees and perched on Ceiriog's tombstone. Doubtless the owl chose that stone because it happens to be one of the tallest there. But to see the strange bird (are not owls always strange?) standing above the poet's grave and staring at me with fixed, round, questioning eyes was a rather moving experience. Thank goodness owls to me are owls and nothing more!

'Unsuitable for Motors'

Possibly you know the beautiful Llyfnant valley? If so you will know the narrow lane that approaches it from the Aberystwyth—Machynlleth road. It winds and climbs over a hill, then drops through woods into the deep cleft of the valley. There are gates across the road at intervals; and there are places where river and lane are squeezed together by rocky walls and cars pass each other with difficulty. For some time past there has been no fingerpost at the entrance to this lane. How wise the highway people are, we thought, not to encourage traffic up a road like that. We flattered them. For now all along the main road has come an absolute deluge of signposts of all sorts, some unnecessarily large, others largely unnecessary. Need I tell you that the lane to Llyfnant valley is now labelled 'Scenic Route'? It is easy to see how such absurdities are perpetrated. Somebody sits planning in a city office a hundred miles away, and soon thousands of motorists are pouring up a lane that is fit only for ponies and traps. Surely if we must have a sign there it had better be 'Unsuitable for Motors'. We have now reached the point in the motoring age where we ought to accept that the car, in large numbers, is incompatible with the beauty and enjoyment of 'fairy glen' valleys and that their lanes should be kept for walkers, ponies and farm vehicles only.

Nest-box Opportunists

Early each morning at this time of year a delightful little song slips into my waking dreams. It comes from the pied flycatcher who every year nests in one of two boxes we have on the sills of our bedroom windows. Three-quarters asleep, I am just aware that the flycatcher is out there singing on top of his chosen box. But then he flies up to perch on the open sash window and sings straight into the bedroom, filling the room with sweet sound. Now I am fully awake and without moving I watch this little black and white bird who comes each April 3,000 miles from Africa to sing at my bedroom window. But not for long this morning. There is a swoop and flurry of alien wings as the flycatcher and an assailant flutter in close combat outside the window. A glimpse of russet feathers tells me that the new arrival is a redstart and I know that for days to come these rival nest-box enthusiasts will be squabbling over one box while the other box is left unguarded. In some years this has been the opportunity for a great tit to nip in and occupy the neglected box, an incident of which Aesop would have made a well-told fable for the instruction of mankind.

Queen Wasps in 1970

Now it is queen wasp time. And queen wasps divide people into two groups, the pest destroyers and the live-and-let-lives. The destroyers claim that if queen wasps are killed in spring then we are all better off in the autumn: no wasps in the jam, no stings, no ruined picnics and our crops of fruit and honey not endangered. So off they sally to where the queen wasps gather, at the flowers of cotoneasters, for example, to tackle them with blunt instruments and poison sprays, no doubt inadvertently killing many harmless insects in the process. We, of the other school of thought, see the queen wasp as a beautiful and fascinating creature. We watch her rasping at the surface of posts and boards collecting material to make her admirable nest. (So many millions of years before man got to it she invented how to turn wood into paper.) We see her swoop hawk-like on flies and know that her many progeny too will destroy vast numbers of flies throughout the summer. In other words we welcome wasps as part of a healthy and robust natural pattern we have no desire to disturb unless really forced to. We would not argue for the conservation of malarial mosquitoes or bubonic rats. But we would argue against destroying animals merely to add a bit more comfort to our already overcomfortable lives. So prosperity to wasps in European Conservation Year.

Country Notice-Boards

Some diligent researcher could write an amusing book on the subject of country notice-boards. For although there is a depressing unoriginality about most of them (I suppose 90 per cent are devoted to a bleak 'Trespassers will be prosecuted' or similar protestations of brotherly love), yet there is commendable if sometimes unconscious humour among the rest. There is, for instance, the sign along the Severn near Welshpool which says 'No Coarse Fishermen'. There are also leg-pulls of the sort reported lately in *Country Life:* a notice on a Devon gate warning people that it was dangerous to enter without protective clothing because the fields there were 'Covered with *taraxacum*'. Only botanists would know *taraxacum* as the common dandelion.

But a notice I saw on a wood in France I did not know whether to take seriously or not. It said *'Pièges à loups'* (wolf traps), but as I was not all that far from Paris, genuine wolves hardly seemed likely, so I risked it and came to no harm. Notices telling motorists to look out for wild boars (*'Attention sangliers'*) are more realistic, except that they leave you wondering whether it is the safety of the boars or the motorists that the fuss is about. The frugal French countryman usually wastes a lot less paint than we do on notice-board verbiage, but the most succinct I remember was outside a very flowery wood; it said simply, *'Muguet interdit'*—literally, 'Lily of the Valley forbidden'. Make of that what you will!

Garden and other Robins

When at last the weather warmed up ever so slightly on Tuesday I took a spade and advanced on the vegetable patch for the first time this year. And from the very moment I started digging, there was a robin watching me from the fence. It was just as if he had been waiting six months for me to come out and dig up worms for him. It's the same with my farming neighbour. He, too, has his 'robins' the instant he starts his spring ploughing. Up and down the field goes his tractor, and as the plough-share turns the earth, a white cloud of black-headed gulls flutter closely behind, diving on the worms the instant they are revealed. Out on the marshy lands along the estuary I see a quite different sort of 'robin.' All the year there are digging machines at work clearing out the miles of ditches. Hour after hour their buckets swing round and empty gallons of mud and water on the banks, along with heaps of wriggling eels. At some time or other a heron more astute that the rest realised that by following a digger all day, he could have the life of Riley. Soon the idea caught on, and now it is an everyday sight to see herons, normally the shyest of birds, almost getting scooped up by the machines in their undignified scramble to snatch the eels. When the digger drivers stop for lunch, the herons wait patiently only a few feet away. Working all day far away in the loneliness of the marshes, the digger drivers no doubt enjoy their herons as much as gardeners love their robins.

Hilda Murrell Remembered, 1987

At the end of our garden stands a row of balsam poplars which, as the leaves unfold, will soon be shedding a sharp fragrance on the air. They have grown fast since we planted them nearly thirty years ago and are now really much too big for the garden. But we shall not be cutting them down because they remind us constantly of the friend from whose nursery we bought them: Hilda Murrell who died four years ago in mysterious circumstances. She was known world-wide as an authority on the old roses. She was a champion of nature conservation and the protection of rural England, especially in her native Shropshire, as well as being a courageous anti-nuclear campaigner. She was also a gifted naturalist who kept a careful and loving record of her daily observations. Since her death some of her friends have made a selection of her journals which have now been published as *The Nature Diaries of Hilda Murrell*, a charming book which is a vivid evocation of the delight she found in the Shropshire countryside, on her many visits to Wales and on her trips to Scotland, Ireland and Mallorca. The diaries are written in an easy-to-read style, and she is at her best when giving us word-pictures of landscapes, birds and especially wild flowers as she passes easily from the lyrical to the scientific and back again. Her own skilful drawings and colour photographs illuminate the text which is edited by her friend Charles Sinker, who introduces the author in a thoughtful and revealing essay. The result is a splendid memorial volume to a quite remarkable woman.

Dinefwr—A Real Welsh Castle

Have you ever visited Dinefwr Castle in Carmarthenshire? Have you even heard of this substantial ruin which from its wooded hilltop looks across the wide valley of the Tywi? Certainly this castle has never achieved much fame but there are indignant Welsh patriots who will tell you that the reason for its neglect, in an English-dominated Wales, is that it was a Welsh not an English castle. Here at the start of the Middle Ages lived the princes of south Wales (sometimes they also ruled the whole of Wales) and it was they who first built a castle here to defend south-west Wales against threats from the east. So in Welsh eyes this is a castle far more worthy of preservation than those at Harlech, Caernarfon and others erected to keep the Welsh in subjection and are therefore symbols of tyranny. At Dinefwr there is not only the castle. There are also its woodlands and a deer park complete with deer. And though the estate in recent years has fallen on hard times all is now changing. The tottering castle will soon cease to totter. Its ruins are being made safe and eventually will be open to the public. The woodlands, devastated by neglect and elm disease, are now being cared for. The reason for this revolution is that the estate has been bought by two eminent organisations, the National Trust and the Dyfed Wildlife Trust, and their rehabilitation schemes are supported by other influential bodies. So, although hitherto you may not have been aware of its historical importance, I think you are going to hear plenty about Dinefwr from now on.

MAY

Cuckoo in the Nest?

Hearing that a forest-worker had found a cuckoo's egg in a hedge-sparrow's nest I went off to the woods this morning in the hope of getting a photograph of it. On my way there I wondered how the cuckoo has acquired the habit of laying in other birds' nests. But it was a problem of human behaviour I came home with. For when I reached the place I found that the discovery of this nest had raised quite a problem of ethics among the men working in that section of the forest. In fact the gang was quite split in two over it.

One side said that the cuckoo's egg ought to be destroyed. They argued that by so doing you take only one life and that instantaneously. Whereas if you do not destroy the cuckoo's egg then you are condemning a brood of young hedge-sparrows to a slow death. But the other side pooh-poohed this attitude as sentimental and pointed out that man was not to blame if nature had to employ such crude means of producing cuckoos; and that anyway it would be very interesting to watch a young cuckoo grow up.

The matter had been discussed between fifteen men throughout one lunch-hour and had then been put to the vote. Six were for not interfering, but nine said the cuckoo's egg ought to be destroyed. And, democracy being what it is, I didn't get my photograph. But which way would you have voted?

A Treasure Re-found

I feel I must record the story—a perfectly true one—of Nancy Jones and her wedding ring. It happened on a hill-farm in Cardiganshire. One day newly wedded Nancy lost her ring while helping to plant potatoes. Friends were summoned and the field was searched long but in vain. Later, when the potatoes were harvested, everyone looked out for the ring but it remained lost. Another year came round and the ploughman kept his eyes open. So did all who worked in the field. The following year the same. And year after year, whoever had business in that field always had Nancy's ring in the back of his mind.

In the course of time the farm changed hands but, as happens in these parts, it went no farther than to cousins. So the memory of the lost ring remained alive until thirty-eight years had passed. Then came a spring day when a man was ploughing the field behind a pair of horses. You must believe me when I tell you that after thirty-eight years he still looked out for the ring, and knew just which part of the field Nancy had lost it in. And this time, when he came there, he found it. He picked it up, put it carefully into his waistcoat pocket, left his horses and ran all the way down to the village to place it triumphantly into Nancy's now ageing palm.

Botanists Befogged

When the Reverend John Evans wrote up his botanical tour of north Wales in 1798 he added as a footnote to one page that in a spot near Ffestiniog he had found a wildflower called the northern rockcress. Now it happens that the northern rockcress is extremely rare thereabouts. So last Saturday members of the Merioneth Field Society went off to try to find this long-lost rarity. After all, we asked, what is a mere century and a half in the existence of a wild plant? (Botanists, you see, are nothing if not optimistic.)

We met at lunch-time in thick mountain mist. And in thick mountain mist we spent the rest of the day. It was very strange to be walking the hills and seeing no natural features until they loomed out of the fog a few yards off: the eerie gleam of a moorland pool fringed with rushes; the sudden menace of great rocks almost overhead before we saw them. So it was that, as the result of a clergyman's after-thought one day in 1798, nearly twenty people spent an afternoon in 1963 floundering about a fog-bound mountainside. But everyone seemed quite happy. For most it was a new and interesting experience. Still, one cannot help being suspicious of some of these old records of rare plants. One cannot help wondering if Mr Evans really did find northern rockcress there. One thing is certain: we did not!

A Hill Walk at Sunset

My shadow was already three times as long as myself as I walked up the slopes of a valley in central Wales. At last I came up to the watershed and found what I was seeking: one of the least noticeable yet most unusual earthworks in the district, nothing more than a low bank a yard wide alongside a shallow ditch. It is so insignificant yet it goes for several miles across the tops and up and down the slopes like some miniature Offa's Dyke. Insignificant yet highly durable, for this small bank and its furrow, made to mark out the empire of the local Cistercian monastery, has lasted six or seven centuries.

The evening was still and cloudless and a golden light lay across the hills while the valleys had gone into shadow. In that rich light all things were redder than is usual, not only the cotton grass and the rushes but also the lone hare that went racing up the turf and a fox that ran out of the heather. In the air was a hovering kestrel, a buzzard and, loveliest of all, a kite: all much ruddier than they are in the white light of midday. With the utmost grace the kite circled and dipped, coming round over me again and again. And when I was back again in the greyness of the valley I could still see him soaring over the hill, now catching the sun redder than ever on his shapely wings.

Leverets in our Kitchen

Some weeks ago two baby leverets, rescued from the ploughshare, were given to us to rear. They were wonderful little creatures. Though so recently born they were well furred, alert, open-eyed, ready to face the world. Each fitted snugly into the palm of a hand and their food was a sip of milk at intervals. But how quickly young animals grow! In a few days their teeth could give us a sharp nip and they were nibbling lettuce leaves. We named them Big and Small, so different were they in size. Their characters were curiously different, too. Big was shy and backward; Small was friendlier and was the first to learn to lap milk and eat lettuce.

Now they are almost hares, very strong, hard-kicking, hard-scratching hares. No longer is it easy to pick them up and fondle them. Not that we have wished to tame them, for they must go back to the wild with the best chances of survival. Their appetite is now great, yet selective. They eat grass and the leaves and flowers of dandelions, but not docks nor daisies. They accept cabbage but much prefer purple-sprouting broccoli and lettuce. They could not have been easier to rear: all along their feeding has never been the slightest problem. The only problems lie ahead: to find somewhere safe to release them and, even harder, to bring ourselves to part with such lovable, gentle-eyed, long-whiskered, softly-furred beauties.

Rare Hawk of the Marshes, 1974

There are few more attractive birds of prey than Montagu's harriers. Lightly they float over marshes and heathlands, the females a rich dark-brown in strange contrast with males that are as pale as herring gulls. But they are sadly rare in Britain now, these harriers. A couple of decades ago you could have said their future was almost promising. After a long bad spell there seemed hope that they might make a come back for they were breeding in quite a few counties. But then came a rapid decline. On a favourite marsh of mine in west Wales I watched a pair for the last time in 1963. From a nearby hill I saw them playing gracefully on the upper air in courtship display. Many weeks later there was the joy of seeing them and two young ones on the wing. But they have never nested there since. Yet, such is human optimism, I have visited the marsh every spring in the hope that the harriers will return. Which brings me writing this in the bright May sunlight with sedge warblers and reed buntings singing all round me. But there are still no harriers. Nor I fear will there ever be again until something is done to stop the destruction of these lovely birds when on migration in the Mediterranean region where they are said to be shot down by trigger-happy sportsmen interested in them only for target practice.

Snowdon's Alpine Flowers

To see moss campion in flower, so my flora tells me, I should seek it in July and August. But when I went to Snowdon in the last week of May, there it was, bright-pink cushions of it scattered along its favourite crevices. Already some of it was going over and I could not see any of it lasting a great while longer. Low growing and so unruffled by the wind, it is a co-operative plant to photograph, unlike the nearby *Dryas* whose large white flowers flutter incessantly in the breeze. In fact the photography of such ever-nodding blooms can be so nerve-racking a test of patience and concentration it would have been much pleasanter to have left the camera at home and taken a more leisurely enjoyment of the varied plants that adorn these crags wherever the rock is suitable.

There was rose-root, some already over, some still in full yellow flower; the beautiful *Antennaria* with its woolly pink and white heads peeping down from high ledges; the mountain sorrel, so pleasing for its round fleshy leaves; three saxifrages, purple (now over, of course), starry (at its best) and mossy (just coming into bloom). Then on the cool rocks of a shadowy cwm, in the company of globe-flowers, alpine bistort and alpine saw-wort, there was the rarest and loveliest treasure of all, the unique little lily called *Lloydia*, its delicate white cups erect above wiry grass-like stems.

'Flore de la France'

When a few months ago a kind friend gave me a nineteenth-century book about the wildflowers of France I had no idea of being able to use it this year. Yet quite unexpectedly here I am in a forest 120 miles south-east of Paris. When I tell you that my home in Wales is at the edge of a peat-bog and that here the wildflowers are those of chalk woodland, you will understand that I am rather out of my depth botanically and that my *Flore de la France* is a very much needed companion.

What is striking is how common some plants are here that are uncommon in Britain. The meadow sage makes blue splashes along the roadsides. That inland sea-holly we call the Watling Street thistle is everywhere. There are quantities of rampions and white rock-roses and twin-flowered honeysuckle. Then there are various spurges, genistas and speedwells that the book and I are doing our best with. But what are quite out of this world are two orchids now in full flower along some roadsides and in woods: the military orchids with their lavender-grey hoods and carmine lips, and the lady orchids which, in contrast, have purple-brown hoods over whitish lips.

So for several perfect days I have enjoyed these limestone flowers. And surely the old book has too. Its yellowing musty pages must be glad to be turning again at last in the sunshine of France.

Colourful Spain

Motoring south on the Continent in ever-improving weather and on ever-worsening roads we amused ourselves by listing the birds seen along the way. In the first quarter of Spain there was little that we had not already seen in France: birds such as serins, orioles, woodchat shrikes and

Bonelli's warblers. But quite suddenly the world changed. Gaudy blue rollers and bee-eaters began to appear along the wires. Hoopoes were everywhere and whenever we halted we heard their monotonous 'oop-oop-oop'. By now willow warblers had been left far behind and in the holm-oak woods there was the thrush-like fluting of the orphean warbler instead.

Black kites became common but it was not till we reached a town with white storks standing tamely along the castle walls and a flock of squealing lesser kestrels in the air above that we felt we were truly in the south. Our first azure-winged magpie was a joyous sight as it rose from the wayside. Finally, a line of cattle egrets flighting to roost against the sunset made us feel we were at last not far from Africa. But even with no birds at all, the wonderful displays of cistuses, whole acres blue with lavender, and asphodels nearly six-feet tall would have made the long trip worth while. They say the spring flowers of Greece are marvellous. They certainly are if they are more colourful than the spring flowers of southern Spain.

Wildlife in the Garden

The rain comes, tall grasses threaten the garden paths and I go out with my scythe. It is slow work. I have not been at it five minutes before I see a strange bumble bee. So back to the house for the field guide to insects and I stand book in hand trying to name my bee as she visits the foxglove flowers. Back to work but again not for long because I notice a little bird fly past steering a load of nesting material towards a rhododendron clump. It is a redpoll and as a redpoll's nest is not something you find every day, I watch to see which bush she dives into. Then repeatedly from our willow tree she carries fluffy seeds to line her nest. I turn again to my scything. Soon I am carrying a pile of vegetation to the compost heap. But when I remove its cover, what do I find but two large snakes coiled up underneath. And as I watch them I am surprised to see two bank voles pop out only a couple of inches from them. I have never thought to see snakes and voles living happily together like this. But it is one of the fascinations of nature that you can often make these little discoveries that give you a new insight into the behaviour of common animals. And you don't need to go outside your garden gate to do it.

What Price a Purple Gallinule? 1966

Two weeks ago I was battling across Spain's splendid new nature reserve on the Coto Doñana in almost overwhelming heat. My feet were scorched and my eyes filled with blown sand as I struggled up and down burning, mountain-sized, very loose dunes. But there were compensations. I passed a pool where a purple heron was feeding its young and I heard the strange voice of the crested coot. On another pool there were red-crested pochards, ferruginous ducks and whiskered terns. And on the way back I had good views of the rare imperial eagle.

Now I am home amid coolness, clouds and rain and I hear of a nearby farmer who is chewing his nails because of ground too sodden for barley sowing. It would be cruel to tell him how in south Spain I saw the corn already tall and golden and that by now they are probably beginning the harvest. All the same I have doubts about Spain in the summer. For after their harvest, what then? Only long months of heat and drought and the world drying up into dust. I am sure that the Coto Doñana is a truly wonderful place from November to May. But in the other half of the year it can be about the hottest, driest place in Europe and I'm sure I couldn't bear it; so give me then the green, soaking hills of Wales even if we are a bit short of imperial eagles and purple gallinules.

Farewell to a Great Conservationist, 1985

This week we heard of the death of the grand old man of nature conservation in Wales. Colonel Morrey Salmon of Cardiff had a splendid innings (he was in his ninety-fourth year) and for very long he fought the good fight for bird protection and the creation of nature reserves with wonderful tenacity. In the annals his name will always be linked with that of the late Geoffrey Ingram, also of Cardiff, because of their pioneering work in bird photography and for their studies of the birds of southern Wales. Their first-class book, *Birds in Britain Today*, which appeared in 1934, is proof of their wide knowledge of England and Scotland as well as Wales. They were fortunate to have lived when they did, and were able to enjoy a countryside as yet unsavaged by all the pollution and habitat destruction which have been such a blight on the post-war world. Indeed, in their younger days there were nightingales nesting commonly in the suburbs of Cardiff. But, for security reasons, Colonel Salmon's greatest achievement in natural history must remain almost unknown to the public, and this came from his devotion to the protection of that most famous of all Welsh birds, the rare red kite. He kept a private chronicle of the fate of every known kite's nest and his meticulous records covering all this century could well be the longest detailed study of a rare bird anywhere in the world. It is sad that possibly the last news he ever received about the red kite was of one killed a fortnight ago by one of those very low-flying jets that are such a curse in the countryside of today.

Wedded to the W.I.

For over thirty years I have belonged to an unofficial, exclusively male club called the WI Husbands. We are the chaps who weekly or monthly see our ladies sallying gaily off to those mysterious institute gatherings where, amid much chat and laughter, goodness knows what larks the dear things get up to. My wife's institute is in a village so small it is hard to believe that a WI branch has held together here for all of sixty-two years. Yet there are the minute books to prove it. Written in many hands and styles, they reveal a marvellous history of parish activities, for nothing much would have happened here over the years without the WI to take the lead. The chronicle reveals the ladies entertaining themselves with fun and games, keep-fit, yoga, folk dancing and coach trips to far-away places. It also shows them in earnest pursuit of knowledge, raising funds for endless good causes, encouraging crafts of every description, caring for nature and the countryside, and pioneering for the common good. I am moved to write about the ladies this week because on Wednesday evening they flung open their doors and invited everybody to an exhibition of how they have spent the years. It was all very impressive, and this month WIs everywhere will be doing something similar as part of a national promotion campaign. One of their leading lights said recently: 'This is the WI, and I am proud to be a member'. And I think there are plenty of chaps like me who would say: 'This is the WI and I am proud to be a WI husband'.

Serpents in the Garden

Every spring in our garden we have a small invasion of grass snakes. Some of them may be as much as four feet long and when you meet these outsize individuals, harmless though you know them to be, it is difficult to avoid a quick tremor of alarm, so fundamental is our fear of all the serpents. Snakes are said to be deaf to many sounds that we can detect, otherwise I'm sure they would rejoice to hear the lawnmower making the first cut of the year. For it's the lawn mowings piled up on the compost heap week after week that makes the garden so popular with grass snakes. In July the females will disappear inside the heap, lay their piles of white eggs and then depart, leaving the heap of rotting compost to do the hatching. Mercifully, that poisonous snake, the adder, does not lay eggs and so has no interest in compost heaps. So although we have a few adders as neighbours they mostly keep outside the fence. One that did try to get in got itself caught in the mesh of the rabbit wire surrounding the garden and I was summoned to deal with it. Gingerly I approached with my wire cutters but the adder showed no fear as I cut it free and carried it back to the wild in a cardboard box. I wish I could relate how I intrepidly picked it up by the tail the way experienced snake handlers do it. But this is a trick I have never yet seen done and until I have I doubt if I'll be brave enough for what sounds a delicate operation.

Nature Wastes Nothing

When I recently fixed a nest-box on one of our bedroom window ledges I thought its most likely occupant would be a blue tit. Sure enough a blue tit was popping in and out of it within minutes. But next day a male pied flycatcher arrived after his long migration from Africa. He showed an immediate interest in this desirable residence and very soon the blue tit was evicted. Then along came another migrant, this time a redstart, and he too decided that this box was the perfect answer to the housing shortage. For the next two days there was many a colourful scuffle until the flycatcher retired from the contest. So last week the female redstart was busy building the foundations of a nest in the box with countless beakfuls of moss, wool and dried grass. Meanwhile we experienced one of life's little tragedies. A garden warbler flew into one of our window-panes and was killed. It depressed us to think that this little bird had flown 2,000 miles to fill our garden with song only to die almost as soon as he got here. His body lay in the garden all day and was found that night by a rat or some other scavenger. All that remained next day was a scatter of feathers. That was just a week ago. This morning I went to see how the redstart's nest was getting on in the box on the window-ledge. It contained four blue eggs neatly cradled amongst the brown feathers of a garden warbler. In nature nothing is wasted.

JUNE

Voices at Dawn, 1960

One morning recently I listened to a dawn chorus of woodland and water birds as I stood under a great riverside cedar in Attingham Park, near Shrewsbury. Nothing remarkable about that, you may say. Yet there was one thing noteworthy: I did not stand there in lyrical solitude but in the company of forty other people. Silently we all listened in the darkness to the awakening of the birds. I felt as if three-thousand years had vanished and we were a primitive people engaged in silent worship of some benevolent power of nature. I found myself thinking of the far-off pagan times when the Welsh people are said to have ceremoniously climbed to their mountain tops to see the sun rise, a practice I am glad to learn still persists—or has been revived—on Snowdon even today.

Another delight of the dawn chorus is that you never know what unexpected bird you may hear taking part in it. For instance, on a farm near Harlech recently someone reported that the dawn chorus in his wood included the exotic notes of a hoopoe. So last weekend an early-morning party of us sat on the hillside above his house. Frankly, we had not much hope. But that only increased our delight when we heard a strange, far-off cry of 'poo-poop' and then saw a hoopoe come flying up to the nearest tree-top and repeat his outlandish note before flapping off towards the hills.

Anglesey Idyll, 1960

Anglesey, I think, must have been a wonderful county before any bridges crossed the strait: then it was altogether secluded, unindustrialised, townless and peaceful. There are parts of it even today that are most refreshingly remote and undisturbed, though not for long, I fear, in view of the triple menace of caravans, atomic stations and industrial overspill. So today rather than tomorrow is the time to go to Anglesey; and the seeker after wild places, birds and plants can still find much to delight in.

There are the cliff-tops of the east, colourful with blue squills, yellow rockroses (common and hoary), bloody cranesbills and green-veined orchids. There are inland marshes and lakes rich with aquatic plants and birds. There are peaty places where you can find the pale heath violet now and the gorgeous marsh gentian later on. The north-west will give you a shingle-beach white for half a mile with the massed flowers of sea-kale. The western cliffs are lively with fulmars and guillemots nesting under slopes yellow and white with cat's ears and sea campions. And in the south are wide reaches of rock, marsh and sand where there are shore plants in great variety, a profusion of orchids, colonies of cormorants and terns, and views across the dunes to that great line of mountain silhouettes that cross the horizon all the way from the Carneddau and Snowdon nearly to the end of the Llŷn peninsula.

Canal Without Water, 1960

I have had many a happy day walking along the banks of country canals, especially those delightful half-disused waterways that wind through the fields and round the little hills of the Welsh border. But last week in Shropshire I found that even a canal without water can be nearly as good, a discovery I made by following for some miles the long-disused canal at Woofferton.

No question of a tow-path ramble here. Instead I walked in the greater seclusion of the dried-up canal bed between grassy banks full of meadow flowers and bushes shouting with greenfinches and lesser whitethroats. Then the canal gets mixed up with a railway line and the two argue together for a mile or two until the canal curves away across a field to the banks of the Teme which it once crossed on what must have been a splendid three-arched aqueduct. But as this is now in ruins, I could follow the canal no farther.

It was here I got into conversation with one well-versed in the region's history. He told me of an ancient wool-traders' mule track that passed nearby on its way from Ludlow to the Severn and he pointed out the faint line it still made across the field we were standing in. So with my bridges broken before me I turned perforce from the canal to this most alluring medieval road, a road I would like to try to follow throughout its length some day.

An Ancient Road across Wales

Shrewsbury, as we all know, is a great centre of roads and rails. To find out why, you have only to turn to the map of Roman Britain, put your finger on Wroxeter, that is Viroconium, just outside Shrewsbury, and you will see how the Romans sent out their roads from there; four roads that go sweeping to the four horizons, going off with the geometrical certitude that betokens unity, power and conquest. One goes straight north for Chester; another straight east, and eventually London-wards; the third goes south-west, delightfully leading you through the Shropshire uplands and on to south Wales.

But it is the fourth road that is my favourite way out of Wroxeter, the one that brings me straight back west into Wales. It is a road I have got to know bit by bit over the years through chancing on it here and there. But lately I have had the pleasure of following it deliberately as far as I could until I lost it on the moors south-east of Pumlumon.

Not that I follow Roman roads because I have any admiration for those who made them. These roads after all were often trails of bloody conquest and the driven slave. So when I follow Roman roads I like to forget the Romans and admire only the quiet woodpaths, the overgrown lanes, the faintly ridged fields and the ancient hedges, trees and gateways these old roads bring to light.

Quest for a Rare Fern

I have just been searching for one of Britain's rarest ferns. It is called the Killarney fern and is said to have been found fifty years ago in one of our local ravines but has not been seen since. You may think it outrageously optimistic to expect to find a plant after so long an interval, but botanists are nothing if not optimistic. The ravine I searched is a magnificent cleft cut into a steep mountainside and shaded from top to bottom by woodland. It climbs for several hundred feet and is full of the thunder of waterfalls, one above the other. The air is permanently damp with spray and sunlight rarely penetrates. In other words it looked just the place for the Killarney fern to be happy in. As I scrambled about the gorge I first got my feet soaked through slipping off a rock into the stream, and then got my head wet while trying to look behind a waterfall. I saw many kinds of ferns and a marvellous assortment of mosses—but not a sign of the Killarney fern. I comfort myself that in several hours I had covered only one-third of the gorge, so I must return one day and continue the search. In such unsuccessful ventures I also find solace in that lovely modern Greek poem about getting to the Island of Ithaca. It is a very long way to Ithaca and there is nothing much to see when at last you get there. But what matters is the quest. As the poem concludes: 'Ithaca has given you the beautiful voyage. Without her you would never have taken the road'.

Links with Wildlife

Years ago I used to disapprove of golf courses, regarding it as iniquitous that so much valuable ground should be wasted on such a fatuous occupation as walking round and giving a little white ball an occasional knock with a stick. But I have long since admitted how wrong I was. For though few of them realise it, these knockers of little balls do more towards the sum total of nature conservation than is done by many naturalists. Admitted the greens and other lawn-like stretches are botanical deserts. But the rough, the lovely rough, is full of treasures. Take our courses along the nearby coast—Borth, Aberdyfi and Harlech in particular. Were it not for the golf-mania the dunes among which these courses lie would certainly be built-up areas or caravan sites. I am prompted to these grateful thoughts by a friend who has just phoned to say that while golfing today he counted 140 lady's tresses. In June he saw 58 bee orchids on the same links. One of our other courses has a large area of marsh orchids, dry banks colourful with pyramidal orchids and a grassy place where flourishes the rare maiden pink. So long life to all golf courses!

Sleepless Nights Abroad

We British naturalists are often regretful because of the limited number of our animal species, but at least we are spared those dreadful Continental nights torn into shreds by a howling cacophony of frogs, crickets and nightingales. Having heard hundreds of nightingales lately in France and Spain I am left marvelling how this species ever got a reputation for beautiful singing. They utter a few soothing phrases, it is true, and now and then they seem about to develop a really splendid tune; but it all collapses into harshness and din. Then there are the mole crickets shrieking; and all those maddening bush crickets. I know that people have written in praise of these sounds but I suspect these admirers never have been campers.

To go camping in southern Europe is not to miss a syllable of all these horrors of which easily the worst are the frogs. Only in the high Pyrenees did we find a camp site entirely free of them. Some merely squeaked and piped and were more or less bearable. But most yelled into the night with rasping, guttural voices that carried half a mile. Of course, as a naturalist, I should have rejoiced at this wealth of pulsating Continental night life, but even naturalists like to sleep sometimes. I admit I found myself longing for the absolute night silence we get in late spring here in the Welsh woods after the owls have finished their silly season.

Two Great Hill-forts

Lately I have been both to Carn Goch and to Pen y Cloddiau, which means that I have visited the two biggest hill-forts in Wales. Pen y Cloddiau is the finest of a chain of several forts that, after 2,000 years, still stand boldly along the Clwydian Hills and have vast prospects over the Dee and Wirral in the east and over the Vale of Clwyd and Snowdon in the west. Carn Goch is many miles south, on a cliffy ridge near Llandeilo in Carmarthenshire. Hill-forts usually consist of earthern banks ringed around a summit. But what distinguishes Carn Goch is its massive stonework. Whatever shape these walls had originally I do not know. But now they consist of loosely heaped rough pebbles like a storm beach along a sea-shore. Like all such easy sources of stone these defences have no doubt been despoiled down the ages but even now they are a decidedly moving sight, rising to twenty feet over long sections of their more than a mile of circumference. Even sober archaeologists have tended to get excited by all the walls, scree and boulders scattered everywhere on this hill and they have fancied they have detected hut circles and chambered tombs where probably none existed. But for me the most intriguing feature is the huge and mysterious mound of stones that stands in the centre of the camp. Carn Goch is decidely a place to let your imagination off its leash.

Flowers of the Mountain Cliffs

I write this perched on a cliff ledge above Llyn y Fan Fach, a lake in south Wales. To my right and left the rocks are bright with flowers and if I look up I see the crag is coloured with blossoms to the top. If I look down, but no, I don't care to look down. I am no rock climber and I dread to have space below my feet. But since, of all our wild plants, it is the mountain ones I love best I just have to make an effort to overcome my fears. Unfortunately cliffs are deceptive. They are far easier to climb up than down. So though I've got to this ledge I know I shall have problems getting down. At the moment, however, I'm all right. The ledge is a yard wide and I can move comfortably in both directions admiring the white cushions of mossy saxifrage and sea campion, and noting more subtle treasures such as green spleenwort, brittle bladder fern, northern bedstraw, rock stonecrop, stone bramble, lesser meadow rue and water avens. There are also many commoner kinds such as early purple orchid, which looks especially handsome blowing in the upland wind, and cowslips, which I have never met with on a mountain ledge before. Loveliest of all are the huge sheets of rose-root, vertical acres of fleshy blue-green leaves and yellow flowers. But now the shades of night are falling fast and I really must fly. If only I could.

Hands off Welsh Peregrines, 1960

Some of the wild birds and animals of Wales have long been unofficially on the export list. Many a Welsh fox, for instance, has been captured and set at liberty in the English hunting shires because of the supposed superior running powers of mountain foxes. Lucklesss Welsh otters and pine martens have from time to time been given or sold to English zoos. More than one Welsh raven has lived out his years as a pinioned cripple at the Tower of London. Other Welsh birds, notably the chough, are illegally sought after by cage-bird fanciers.

But over the centuries the most exported Welsh bird must have been the peregrine. In the hey-day of falconry certain eyries were held in great repsect as annual producers of particularly fine birds. It is recorded how in Tudor time a particular Welsh cliff produced such excellent falcons that 'the great Minister Burleigh sent a letter of thanks for a present of a cast of hawks from this place'. Falconry is now being revived and only last week I received a letter from a Shropshire falconer asking my help in getting him a young peregrine. I had to point out to him that Welsh peregrines are not all that numerous, that their numbers are probably declining and that in any case I felt that a peregrine, surely the very essence of wildness and freedom, should be allowed to stay wild and free.

A Nightjar Interviewed

There were two of us as we walked up the woodpath, the forester who had discovered the nest and I. It was while clearing rhododendrons that the nest had been found by seeing a bird flutter off a patch of ground where no bird had been visible. And now as we gently approached her she was still hard to see, though we knew exactly where to look. From six paces she was a shapeless clod of earth, only the pale slit of her almost closed eye telling us which end of her was her head.

As we very slowly stepped nearer she made no move whatever. Then she was right at our feet, still lying there, her eyes still slits, trusting even now in her camouflage though we stood above her, staring down at her. And now she was no longer a piece of earth but a very beautiful bird whose plumage was the subtlest patterning of greys, blacks, whites and browns. We stood above her, talking softly about her, wondering what aeons of accident and change had gone into the forming of every wonderful feather. I think we could have bent down and touched her, perhaps even held her in our hands. But we did not want to, and withdrew as quietly as we had come, happy to have been so close to this bird of the summer woods which had brought to us a touch of the magic of Africa.

A Plod Across the Wilderness

On Wednesday I pushed aside all books and papers and went for a walk across some hills about twenty-five miles north of here. Normally I am quite well behaved and keep to the footpaths but there I could find no path to follow. For this was the great moorland called Migneint, whose name translated from the Welsh suggests bogs and morasses and my feet were wet in less than fifty yards. After a couple of very slow miles I came to a pair of shapely lakes that lie in a wild hollow over-hung by great crags and screes. Perhaps someone ought to write a book in praise of screes. They are so neglected, yet they make a huge contribution to the majesty of mountain scenery. And as habitats for certain specialised kinds of wildlife they must be unique. Where else do plants and animals have to cope with such difficult living places as these millions of sometimes shifting little stones? From the lakes I decided to take the hard way back, making straight up the scree. And what a mistake that was. It was a scramble I might have enjoyed if the weather had held. But half-way up I was deluged with sudden rain. Have you ever been half-way up a vast scree in heavy rain? I don't recommend it. In the event I had to retreat and came tamely back to the road by way of a sheep track. But though I had a weary plod I would not like this spongy Migneint ever to change. It is one of the last bits of wilderness Wales and as such ought to be cherished. And since it now belongs to the National Trust, all should be well.

Problems on the Beacons

You don't need to be a mountaineer to get a lot of pleasure out of mountains. For instance, if you drive south from Brecon along the Cardiff road you soon climb out of the leafy greenness of the Usk valley and there before you is a high, challenging barrier of treeless summits. If, after a few miles, you then turn off to the right at a sign that says Mountain Centre, you find yourself in a lane which lifts you quickly to a spacious upland rich in prehistory and panoramas. Up here on the moorlands, the Brecon Beacons National Park has a fine visitors' centre that was a pioneer in such things when it was opened in the 1960s. Here you can learn all about the region's past, its geology, geography and natural history. Or you can simply sit looking across to the north face of the Beacons, so beautifully sculpted by the forces of natural erosion.

The Beacons are in my mind because I was there in the lovely sunshine last Wednesday, but I was looking at a different sort of erosion. I attached myself to a group who were concerned with the problem of footpath wear and tear. On all the world's most visited hills, unless really good remedial measures are effected, the trails get ever wider and more squalid. On the Brecon Beacons the problems are quite awesome and I came away full of admiration for the hardy souls who struggle to keep the tracks in repair, probably supported by far less manpower and resources than were available to the Romans when they made their very similar paved road across these uplands nearly 2,000 years ago.

An Island Safeguarded, 1980

Nature conservation receives some horrible knocks from time to time and lately one of the most severe hereabouts has been the loss of a biggish stretch of heather moor, a place rich in birds, insects and plants. In its stead we shall have yet another dismal blanket of spruces to add to the spreading gloom of all the other plantations. Mercifully there are compensations. Just now, for instance, there are joyful sounds reaching us from the north-west of Wales where a group of enthusiasts who two years ago had not a penny between them, have succeeded miraculously in raising over £200,000 to buy and endow the charming island of Bardsey. The initial inspiration behind this achievement came from a small band of devotees who ran the island's bird observatory. With enormous optimism and zeal they set out to recruit as many allies as possible and very quickly the money came flowing in from charities, trusts, official bodies and private individuals. Until then no one had realised how deeply cherished this island is in so many quarters, both Welsh and English. Its religious traditions are strong. In its pattern of little fields it preserves a way of farming life mostly gone from elsewhere. It is a haven for sea birds and many other forms of marine life. Above all it is beautiful, peaceful and swirled round by fearsome waters. And now, thanks to all who have struggled to make this possible, its future is secure against all exploiters.

Friends among the Lepidoptera

Forgive the name-dropping but I do like people to know that among my acquaintances are the Queen of Spain and the Duke of Burgundy. I first met the Queen of Spain in Andalusia. She was sun-bathing in a quiet retreat among the cork oaks and proved rather shy. She did however permit me to take her picture at a respectful distance by telephoto lens—one of the loveliest creatures I have ever been privileged to photograph. My connection with the Duke of Burgundy is rather more tenuous. In a way I know him well for I have several specimens of his family in a collection bequeathed to me by an old naturalist who got them from Dorking in Surrey. But I have not yet actually met him in the flesh. I have looked for him hereabouts but he is still elusive and I fear he has no special love of Wales. Probably our climate suits him not much better than it would the Queen of Spain who would quickly perish in our long cold rains. Besides, his favourite food, the foliage of the cowslip, becomes ever scarcer as our meadows get more and more 'improved'. In any case in these democratic days maybe we should not aspire to hob-nob with aristocrats but be content with footmen, lackeys, rustics and even sharks. After all they include in their ranks some of the most delicately beautiful of all our moths.

Nature along the Narrow-gauge

Being anything but a narrow-gauge railway enthusiast I felt a little fraudulent in accepting an invitation to attend the recent twenty-first birthday celebrations of the Talyllyn Railway. But accept I did and duly turned up at Tywyn where, after speech-making and tape-cutting, the little train went steaming away inland towards the hills. Time slipped back a century as we rattled our leisurely way up the valley with ever lovelier views of wooded slopes rising to mountains beyond. There were other delights as well. There were all the primroses, bluebells and stitchworts along the banks. And there was the pleasure, because of the gentleness of the pace, of being able to name even the mosses on the dripping walls of the cuttings. Half-way we stopped long enough to stroll through woodlands to a first-class waterfall and hear the songs of redstarts, wood warblers and pied flycatchers. Then beyond the upper terminus station we were privileged to steam part way along a so far uncompleted extension of the line, so getting a view of a waterfall I had never seen before. So I ended the return journey having ticked off sixty-two birds on my day's list, observed a splendour of scenes and wild-flowers and collected a new waterfall.

Squirrel at the Window

A grey squirrel has discovered that the ledge outside our window is a lovely warm spot. He sits there and goes through fascinating antics in the cause of washing, grooming and scratching, all of which, if we approach carefully, we can watch from only twelve inches away. Perhaps someone will explain to me why mammals and birds not used to windows cannot as a rule see through them. It is a truly strange experience to see the eyes of this squirrel apparently looking straight into mine yet not really seeing me at all. What then do they see? Reflections? But if that were so, surely the squirrel would react at the sight of his own image? In spring when we have pied flycatchers nesting in a box on the window-ledge the male spends hours fluttering at his reflection. But this squirrel evidently does not see his, though maybe if he comes often enough he will learn to look at us through the glass the same as a cat or a dog does. Another point of interest: his colour. In the bright sun he is mostly a rich red-brown and his only really grey parts are his limbs and the long outer hairs of his tail. If many grey squirrels are as red as this it is no wonder I receive so many reports of red squirrels in this district where I have not seen one myself for many years.

Dragonfly Splendours, 1969

Why go to the royal investiture of the Prince of Wales for pageantry and splendour when all you need to do is sit on the side of any ditch and watch the dragonflies? Take that big one with the broad flat body, for instance. He really is on parade. Constantly he patrols along the ditch, turns at the end of his beat and repasses in front of you as if determined you shall miss nothing of the beauty of his powder-blue body. And his acceleration is wonderfully effortless as he suddenly changes from a slow ambling flight to a speed as quick as a dart. Another of these hawk-like dragonflies is the common aeshna. He is worth seeing for his size alone and when he catches the light you see vivid blue flashes all down his length. Then there is that slender little bright-blue one. Often as he plays about over the water, his transparent wings are so invisible he looks like an azure needle hanging horizontally in the air. Another species has brightness only on the end of his tail. So all you may see of him is a blue spot zigzagging mysteriously over the water. If emerald is your colour there is the green lestes whose body gleams like metal. But most gaudy of all is the demoiselle agrion whose entire wings scintillate with greens, blues and purples. Next week, Prince Charles in all his glory will not be arrayed like one of these.

Where Have All the Cowslips Gone?

Now it is cowslip time. Or it ought to be. It should be possible this week to walk in the fields and see the richer meadows yellow with this wild flower that is among the loveliest of those of spring. But those days have gone. If you know of a cowslip field today you are one of the lucky ones. When the *Flora of the British Isles* was published in 1952, the cowslip was described as 'locally abundant'. That could not be said truthfully of many districts today. In one generation of farmers the old herb-rich meadows have gone so almost completely that nature conservationists now have to write letters in country newspapers asking if anyone knows of fields where orchids or primroses still exist. Today these plants survive mainly in the wilder country churchyards or on those rare lane banks that are not assaulted by cutting machines; or in little unreclaimed corners of farmland. As time passes these odd bits of uncultivated land get more and more precious as havens for wild plants and animals. So every farmer with the slightest sympathy for conservation should see to it that his land includes at least one neglected corner. This will not break him financially.

Summer Comes

This is the week when I end my woodland walks. I love the wood until, quite suddenly in late June, it becomes dark-green and weighed down with leaves and rather silent. The cuckoo has called for the last time and gone. What birds remain are family parties squeaking remotely in the tree-tops and very hard to see. So now I take to the fields where the meadow browns are just beginning to fly. Along the hedge a scarlet tiger moth catches the sun on its brilliant wings. Puss moth and eyed-hawk caterpillars are chewing madly at willow leaves along the railway bank. They almost grow as you watch them. A sparrowhawk flies across the fields and straight to her nest in the larches, carrying food in her talons. On the hill, right up in the heather zone, green woodpeckers are seeking ants among the rocks: for even woodpeckers get weary of woods at this season. If I go out to the estuary I find that there too the world has changed this week. The heronry, a compact little city of birds these four months past, is now a dissolving community. Young herons are scattering all over the saltings and soon every nest will be empty.

The brilliance has faded off the plumage of drake mergansers and now a female floats down-stream leading the year's first duckling brood. So summer is really here. And it looks like rain.

Pterodactyls Everywhere

A feature of life this century has been the ever-growing popularity of the open air movement. And along with it has come a demand by people to be informed about all aspects of the countryside, including its natural history. So books are bought, television is watched, radio listened to and much information acquired. But when people venture out of doors to apply their knowledge anything can happen. Only this week I was with a party of city schoolchildren being shown round a nature reserve. Suddenly a heron flew over and an excited little girl shrieked: 'Look, a pterodactyl!' Well, let us forgive her. Herons, after all, are indeed primitive-looking fowl. But we can't escape the fact that a lamentable gulf exists between this child's evidently considerable book learning and her knowledge about nature in the field. Yet, as I found in the next two hours, all these children, many of whom had never even seen a chaffinch before, learned to identify birds very quickly once they were pointed out. The lesson of all this is simple. What people new to the countryside need is not only books and trail leaflets but personal guides as well. For some years now, notably in the Pembrokeshire Coast National Park, field tours by experts have been conducted. But there are still many districts where no such facilities exist. Until they do, I'm afraid that most people are doomed to go on seeing pterodactyls everywhere they go.

Welsh Poppies take to the Hills

Time now to say goodbye to the garden flowers of early summer. The Welsh poppies, for instance. For many weeks they have been a touch of welcome along the paths but now they are nearly all in seed. In our garden we have the usual two colours: some poppies a lovely clear yellow, others an attractive orange. Yet though they grow entirely mixed up with each other they seldom hybridise, despite being varieties of the same species. Having had them in the garden for thirty years, I wish now that I had kept an annual record of how many were yellow and how many were orange, because it seems to me that the relative numbers have fluctuated greatly over the years. One guess I would make is that yellow-flowered parents never produce orange-flowered descendants and vice versa. A quality that Welsh poppies have, if the conditions suit them, is persistence. They have powerful roots and if they get established in rock gardens they can spread alarmingly. But it is not really in gardens that the toughness of this delightful plant is most convincingly demonstrated. I climbed one of our local mountains this week and when I got up to 2,000 feet I found the flowers of early summer were just reaching perfection, including the Welsh poppies, which were all yellow, by the way, no sign of orange ones. Up there they were living a really hard life and competing successfully with many deep-rooted alpines. Yet why not? After all, our humble Welsh poppy is closely related to those aristocratic blue poppies which grow I don't know how many thousands of feet up in the Himalayas.

A Precious Mid-Wales Wilderness

Last weekend I set out to walk across what I knew by hearsay to be one of the least frequented moorlands in Wales. It is a high, level plateau which on the map looks just perfect for a good day's walk. But as soon as I had climbed high enough to look across this wild upland I realised that although it stretched for only twelve miles I hadn't a hope of getting across it. All experienced hill-walkers know this sort of ground. It consists of mile after laborious mile of peatbog overgrown by huge tussocks of moorgrass where you stumble and flounder along at about half a mile an hour and quickly get hot, tired and bad-tempered. So I abandoned my walk and was quite content to sit on a warm rock in the sun and enjoy the view over this trackless waste. As I waited I could hear distantly across the moor the gentle songs of golden plover and dunlin, two birds whose wilderness habitats are ever-threatened by exploitation or disturbance. So although I am in favour of public access to moorlands I am happy to think that there are still a few quite large stretches that are never likely to attract even the most adventurous rambler, pony trekker or that latest menace, the cross-country motorbike rider. Peatbogs in the past have not had much of a press. But in these days of nature conservation they have become more highly valued because so many have been destroyed by agriculture or forestry. The few still surviving deserve to be treated as the holiest of holy places.

Flora of the Unspoilt Mountains

Wednesday was a perfect day for the hills, sunny yet cooled by a north wind and with wonderful visibility right across Snowdonia. I went clambering with botanical friends up steep slopes to those lowest skirts of the mountain cliffs where the vegetation is made especially luxurious by the mineral-rich water that seeps perennially from deep inside the rocks. The alpine flora is now at its best, the grey rocks splashed with vivid patches of yellow, pink and white with many other colours to be seen if you look more closely. It is a comforting thought that in these days, so cursed by pollution and the destruction of nature, we can still go to the mountains and find a world looking as beautiful and rich in wild plants as it was when it began to be visited by the botanists of three centuries ago. Since those pioneering days our alpine vegetation has been ever more closely studied, but there remains a whole range of unanswered questions in connection with the ecology of plants. For instance, on the mountain we climbed yesterday, which is quite close to Snowdon and very rich in species, there seems to be a complete lack of several alpines that are abundant on Snowdon itself. Notable among these are purple saxifrage, moss campion, spring sandwort and alpine meadow-rue. But why are they absent? On Wednesday we were not greatly worried by such mysteries. We were too lost in wonder not only at the alpine plants but also at the colourful sheets of globe-flowers, water avens and other beauties which until fifty years ago were a great adornment of the wet meadows of the lowlands.

JULY

Cloudberry in Decline?

Cloudberry, an unprickly sort of bramble that grows in peaty bogs, belongs mostly to the remote north of Europe, Asia and America, but its range comes far enough south to bring it into Scotland and northern England, and it even has a slender hold on Wales as far south as nearly to the Severn, for it is plentiful among the heather around 2,000ft near the top of Moel Sych, the highest summit of the Berwyn. It is a plant that has gathered some fame there over the centuries and is traditionally associated with one Dogfan, an early local saint to whom a quart of cloudberries was given as an annual thank-offering.

But the Berwyn cloudberries must have fallen on bad days since, for if you go up there today you will be lucky to find it even flowering, let alone producing fruit enough to fill a saint's quart pot. In fact, a local landlord (whether from a curious sense of humour or zeal for science, I know not) used to offer five shillings (25p) to anyone bringing him a single berry. I have often wondered just how many centuries it is since the cloudberry became such a shy fruiter on the Berwyn. But now I think the change must be pretty recent, for I find a traveller in the 1790s reporting on 'the Berwyn Mulberries' as if they were common: 'They are considered by the natives as powerful anti-scorbutics and held in high esteem for tarts, &c.'

Who Remembers Bushell?

We crossed the hill with its delightful view over marsh and estuary to the sea. Then through knee-high grass and nettles to where, half-way down the slope, there was a dark, overgrown hollow in the shadow of a lone tree. 'There it is, that is Bushell's Well,' said my guide. But he had no idea at all who Bushell might have been. I peered into the dripping grotto cut into the rock exactly as a mine-level is cut. So there it was, Bushell's Well, perhaps the only object in the whole district still commemorating the once great Thomas Bushell who came here in the King's name three centuries ago to salvage the abandoned silver mines. This he accomplished with enormous success, mining deeper that anyone had before and ingeniously overcoming countless engineering problems.

When his master, Charles I, was hard-pressed in the Civil War, Bushell literally made money for him from the silver of the Cardiganshire mines. Even so the war was lost and Bushell, who had been so powerful in the land, had to flee. Success and great repute are flimsy stuff. No doubt Bushell would have been surprised could he have foreseen that 300 years later his name would be known to the local people not for his mining achievement nor the rare honour he had enjoyed of running a royal mint on the coast of Wales, but as the name of a well he once dug in a hillside.

A Change for the Better?

Walking up a long, winding Merioneth valley last week I came at last, two miles beyond where the woods ended, to a ruinous house by a stream, a house so ancient-looking it could have passed for some long-decayed hospice of the medieval time. But a shepherd I met later, who called the place Hafoty Bach, said he remembered when people lived there. The name means 'the little summer home' and were it not for the invention of the Land-Rover the house would still have a roof on it and the shepherd would be summering there yet. As it is, he can live ten miles away down the valley and can tend his sheep by occasional expeditions to the uplands. It is the same story all over the mountain region. A whole people has drained off into the valleys; houses, even roads disappear; a way of life has ended.

Poking about the nettle-girt ruins of this little summer home I disturbed two hares that raced off up the hill. Redstarts, flycatchers and wagtails had nests in the walls. A ring ouzel chattered at me from a byre roof. A pine hanging over the house had a great nest in it with two large young buzzards that looked down at me with intently glaring eyes. There were barn-owl pellets in the bedrooms and ferns bristling out of the chimney. So nature moves in as man moves out. Should we regret the change or not?

Heat-wave Hawk-moths, 1959

What wonderful energy the humming-bird hawk-moths have. Through the whole length of a fine day, or so it seems, they slip and dart from flower to flower, hovering a second or two before each as they probe it for its sweetness, never settling or resting anywhere. Nor are they nearly so dependent on sun and warmth as butterflies are, for sometimes you can see them still feeding in quite cold, rainy weather.

I had never seen one of these non-stop moths at rest until one day last autumn I took a mean advantage of one when I saw him plunge headfirst into the trumpet of a gentian. As he emerged I caught him in the cup of my hands and when I opened them he stayed a moment on my palm, just long enough for me to be able to admire his strong-looking, dark grey fore-wings, barred in black, the reddish hind-wings and the curious, hairlike tufts on the sides of his body. But powerful as these moths look, one of them managed to get himself tangled in a spider's web and would have been seized by the spider had I not been quick to rescue him. When I see how delightful these little humming-bird moths are to watch I wish the bigger, more colourful hawk-moths also flew by day instead of by night.

The Blight of Tourism

A little Pembrokeshire stream flowed down a narrow green valley through fields and under woods to the sea. Just behind the shore the land flattens and there the stream once spread to form a watery level bright with yellow flag irises, meadow sweet and water buttercups. Here sedge warblers had their nests and chattered at the occasional holiday-makers who had walked to this quiet cove down the long winding unmotorable lane from the main road.

That was five years ago. Since then the lane has been straightened, widened and metalled. Scores of car-loads of people now come daily to the shore. The place of the flag irises and the sedge warblers has been cleared and drained to make a car park. There is an ice-cream kiosk, litter bins, lavatories. So progress goes on. Everybody gets a car. Everybody rushes to the coast. Everybody picnics on it, camps on it, wants to put chalets, caravans, houses, even new towns on it. There is the serious danger of the whole of our coast—national parks included—being eventually ringed by a nasty thin ribbon of development. But who cares? Only that small-voiced minority who are always being told we cannot put the clock back. But once we have destroyed them we cannot put the flag irises and the sedge warblers back either. We may be marvellous at raising our standard of living. But what about the standard of life itself?

The Year turns at Lammas

In May the oaks were yellow, in June a soft green, but in July they turned the darkest, sombre green. Then, as August came near, the ends of the boughs bore new leaves, pale-green or coppery-red: the annual output of Lammas shoots. Lammas, once so well-known a date, has little or no meaning to younger generations in this part of the world. It was once a day of harvest festival (Loaf-Mass) and a fair-day. It had weather associations also. If a goose at Lammas fair was seen to pick up a straw, storms would surely follow—a pretty safe prediction for August in north Wales. 'Lammas floods' is a term still in use amongst older people hereabouts.

On Lammas day or very soon afterwards, the swifts depart with astonishing accuracy of time-sense. And with equal regularity the willow warblers, mostly silent the past few weeks, resume their song. I have also heard the Lammas song of willow warblers in trees by Lake Lucerne and I presume they come back into song at the same time right across Europe and Asia. But this new burst of singing soon dies away as the birds move off south. As well as a migration of birds we can imagine a migration of song as these countless warblers pass down into the tropics. For the song of the willow warbler is one of the delights of the central African bush in October and November.

Know Your Naturalists

The various species of naturalists are easily recognisable in the field even at great distances. Bird-watchers are statuesque, sky-scanning, binocular-wielding and all elbows. Insect-hunters are more lithe and active, identifiable by their sudden gazelle-like leaps after flying prey. But if you see a party of people solemnly crossing a heath or a dune with shoulders hunched and heads bowed in apparent misery you may suspect they are botanists. If they are, you have only to watch for a few minutes, for they have certain field characters which are diagnostic. For instance, the flock usually has a leader who, after a few minutes, stops, crouches and peers intently into the vegetation. This is a sign for the rest to gather round him in the typical posteriors-up stance of the successful plant-seeker. With a little practice this posture can even be used as a rough means of identification of the actual plants under examination. For example, the more posterior and the less head visible, the smaller the plant. So the other day I saw a trio of botanists so bent over that they could only have been seeking the very tiniest of our plants. And so indeed they were, for when I went over to them I found them bent in admiration over a mixed colony of *Centunculus* and *Radiola,* none of which, although nearing maturity, was more than half an inch high.

Past and Present in the High Carneddau

I write this sitting on the high crags above one of the many fine lakes in this part of Snowdonia. I look down upon a steep and beautiful wood which because it is growing on mineral-rich volcanic rocks, has an abundance of interesting wildflowers and ferns. A surprising plant here is the wood vetch that clambers generously over rocks and heather, its delightful leaves and showy clusters of purple-veined cream flowers hanging out into space. Below the wood, in damp pastures sloping to a lake, are spotted and fragrant orchids and in a week or two there will be that delicate beauty, the grass of Parnassus.

This land between the Carneddau and the Conwy river is a wide upland shelf quite perfect—so cool and fragrant—for summer living, but just too high and remote for many people to live on it all the year. These days, I mean. For you cannot go far without realising that man has used this region much more in the past. There are the decayed walls of houses, the outlines of ancient cultivations, and almost abandoned churches that stand alone in fields and leave you to reconstruct in your imagination the communities they once served. There is so much of man's past to sit and think about in a place like this. But man lives in the present also and if I do not move smartly down into the valley I shall miss the post with this diary!

Skomer, 1961

To go to Skomer as I did one day last week is to set foot on an island which man, though he has found some use for it down the ages, has now virtually handed back to nature. Modern man will not live all the year round on these high, gale-swept, cliff-girt islands of the west. But primitive man loved them as places of security in a dangerous world, and I hope, lived and tilled on Skomer for many long and peaceful generations. But in after years the Vikings, living by war and plunder, used these Welsh islands as impregnable bases for raids upon the mainland. For the Normans Skomer was little more than a place to farm rabbits and sea-birds and graze a few animals in summer: and so things went on for centuries.

Modern man has farmed the island with varying success, but not in this century. The farm buildings in the centre of the island stand gaunt and ruinous. The fields have gone back to thistles, ragwort and bracken. Today, when you stand on this island-plateau, bleak and high above the streaming tides, and see the mist gathering about the tors of igneous rock that are scattered on its moor-like surface, the place seems utterly primeval. You feel no surprise that, apart from the ruined farmhouse, the most striking man-made features of the island are even now the walls that primitive man set round his little fields two or three thousand years ago.

A Dolphin Corps de Ballet

The other day, sitting on rocks by the Welsh sea, I was startled by a shrill repeated whistling. It came from the sea, not, it seemed, from a distance but from close at hand. Quickly I searched the water for animal or bird. There was nothing. The sunlit green waves surged in and broke in whiteness up the rocks but there was nothing alive there. Anyway, no bird has a long, shrill whistle like that, not even the dunlin. I thought of otters but their whistle is quite different.

The whistling went on, shriller, louder. I could tell myself quite certainly now that it came from the water immediately below me. I stared and stared and got more and more excited seeing nothing. Then, quite suddenly, apparition of delight, a dolphin and then another, then a whole eruption of dolphins came boiling up out of the depths and rolled and played a few yards from me; silently now for their whistling was, I think, submarine only.

I have often had porpoises surface pretty close to me, but to have dolphins so near and dolphins whistling was new. Then I was astonished to see one of these great beaked creatures not once but several times leap from the water, white belly upwards, and fall heavily upside down on to the back of the dolphin next to it. So they leapt and sported as they made gradually away up the coast. Then quite abruptly there was not a sign of them.

Enter the Giant Hogweed, 1966

Man is mixed in his feelings about umbellifers. Some he fears: such as the evil-smelling hemlock with ominous, purple-spotted stem. Some he hates: especially the ground-elder which year after year defeats him in the perennial border. Some uplift his heart: the delicate green fernery and white lace-work of the cow parsley; the yellow delight of wild parsnip; the graceful little pignut and burnet saxifrage. Some he finds good to dose himself or for flavouring his food: parsley, fennel, spignel, sweet cicely, lovage, caraway, coriander, angelica, dill. Some, like parsnip and carrot, he wolfs in quantity. But though he welcomes many into his kitchen gardens, who can blame him if there are few that he happily allows into his flower gardens? Too many of them have dangerous, elbowing, ground-elder qualities.

So in our garden this year we are rather stricken with nerves. Outside our windows we have planted several specimens of the biggest umbellifer of all, truly named the giant hogweed. They have grown with fairy-tale speed and are now ten feet tall with creamy umbels a yard across. They have the added merit of attracting lots of insects, which in their turn attract many birds. In fact, their huge flat flower-heads are natural bird-tables, supplying their own food. And how many bird-tables attract willow warblers, chiff-chaffs and flycatchers? But many flowers mean many seeds. So, we wonder, are we in for a day of reckoning?

More Hogweed Doubts

We were becoming afraid of the giant hogweeds we had planted in our garden. They looked so huge and fecund we feared we were in for everlasting trouble. But after last Saturday's 'Country Diary' we got a letter from a kind-hearted reader. 'Don't worry about the giant hogweed,' he wrote, 'I never see them but in ones or twos.' We took courage. Besides, we said, this is a plant esteemed by the best authors. Gertrude Jekyll, for instance. Still, we had to admit, maybe Gertrude never thought in terms of gardens as small as ours. Indeed, looking up her actual words we found that she thought it would look excellent 'about old water-mills'.

So gloom again. On top of which came Wednesday's post bringing a letter from another reader with very definite views about giant hogweed. 'I am writing to warn you that this plant can be very dangerous. Earlier this year we cut back a lot of it and our children played with the huge leaves. It happened to be hot and the children were wearing few clothes. Two days later they were covered with a rash and huge blisters formed, up to four inches long and half an inch high.' All of which leaves us in some panic!

More Hogweed Condemnation

More about giant hogweeds. The Montgomeryshire reader who reported that his children came up in huge blisters as a result of playing with these plants has had corroboration from letters I have had from people in Cambridgeshire, Cheshire and Essex describing the same effects on children there. (The plants evidently provide excellent weapons for mock battles.) Other readers point out that two similar umbellifers are known to irritate the skin, the common hogweed mildly and wild parsnip severely. It is significant that the children who fell foul of giant hogweed had one circumstance in common—hot and sunny weather. So bright sunlight may well be a necessary factor in the trouble. This is borne out by an article in *The Lancet* of 29 August 1964, describing how five Brighton boys were badly blistered after playing with leaves of wild parsnip followed by swimming and sunbathing. In the following week's *Lancet* was a letter describing similar effects from giant hogweed. So, as one of my correspondents states, it looks as if the juices of these plants render the skin, probably of fair people especially, more transparent to ultra-violet light. The blisters are protective, formed to prevent the passage of excessive ultra-violet light which would do further damage to the tissues. Let me now thank the senders of all these thoughtful hogweedy letters. And especially my latest correspondent; for he reports that he is now experimenting with eating giant hogweed. I may not get another opportunity of thanking him.

Despite all, the Hogweed lives on, 1967

When a friend wrote recently and added a p.s.—'How's that plant?'—I knew that he meant the giant hogweed I described in this diary a year ago and which brought in more letters than anything I have ever mentioned.

Last year's plants duly disappeared but this year one has come up in a different place. It sowed itself at a path edge and for several weeks looked harmless enough. But suddenly it stretched out huge arms all round and now the path is quite blocked. Meanwhile the main stem is shooting up with equal speed and will soon be expanding massive umbels. I see it through the window as I write. Its ten-foot, soon to be twelve-foot, purple stem stands rigid as a flag-pole while shrubs all round are tossing in the wind. Fortunately, thanks to last year's correspondents, we are now forewarned against its poisonous powers. So if we do have to cut our way past it we shall keep its acrid juices from our skin, especially if the sun is hot. Not that I expect we shall harm it, for we know that its life is short. No plant I know grows quicker or dies down with such haste. It is something to admire while it lasts, a plant to enjoy for its stature, beauty and geometry and for all the insects and small birds, especially warblers, that will be visiting its flowers next week.

Serpents in the Garden

Gardeners who are devoted to their compost heaps all love a hot July when the weed jungle goes mad and they can scythe it down triumphantly and stack it in mountainous piles which soon begin to rot and warm up inside. This is the moment when every year the grass snakes come into our garden. They soon find their way to the compost heap, and for a few days they lie there, especially early in the morning. And if we happen to disturb them they do not panic. Instead, they pour themselves with slow dignity into a hole that leads down inside the heap. Sometime during the next two or three weeks they lay many eggs, made of a parchment-like material that must be extremely tough to withstand the putrefaction that goes on in the pile. Then one day, the heap is crawling with snakelets about six inches long which quickly disperse all over the garden. Then we thank heaven that they are only harmless grass snakes. We are grateful, too, that adders do not lay eggs and therefore have no interest in compost heaps. The idea of sharing the garden with scores of baby adders does not bear thinking about, for right from birth they have poison in their fangs. Which reminds me of a friend of mine who once put his finger into a weaverbird's nest in Africa and got bitten by a tiny and rare kind of snake that had taken up residence there. Fortunately, he was a snake-watcher as well as a bird-watcher, and was delighted to meet a new species, even though his arm ached for the next few hours.

A Pushing New-Zealander

When I reported here recently about alien squirrels being seen improbably high on the Welsh mountains, a correspondent wrote asking about alien plants up there. During the summer she noticed several along mountain trails, the most striking being a tomato plant growing happily at 1,400 feet above sea level. But in view of the huge numbers of tomatoes which must be taken on picnics I suppose it is surprising that the whole British countryside is not overgrown by a jungle of tomatoes. For our domestic tomato is uproariously germinative (unlike a certain wild species which, if I remember correctly, will germinate only if it has passed through the gut of a giant tortoise of the Galapagos or some other unlikely creature). There is, however, one remarkable little alien plant which has surpassed all others as a coloniser of our mountains. When back in 1930 the New Zealand willow- herb was first recorded in Snowdonia at 900 feet its finder, aware of its powers of speedy proliferation, said that he expected it would soon be spreading elsewhere. How right he was. It made progress worthy of the Triffids and today it is even on the highest ledges, elbowing its way amongst the toughest arctic-alpines and still advancing rapidly. In fact, I half expect someone will write to tell me that, as is often the way with aliens, this little invader is doing far better here than in its native New Zealand.

Summer at its height

Now the bog is white all over with the seeding heads of cotton sedge. Sundews are busy catching flies, even a few butterflies, on their sticky, sensitive leaves. Look on the sallows and there are strange-shaped caterpillars that lash at you with threatening, harmless tails: not as big as puss-moth larvae they are wittily known as kittens. Look closer and you find the yellow-green eggs of eyed hawk-moths stuck singly on the underside of the leaves. In the marshes purple orchids of dubious parentage glow darkly among the rushes. On the estuary, families of infant shelducks and mergansers are sailing like fleets in formation. Each day in the trees round the garden there are fewer voices in the dawn and evening chorus. Our mistle thrush has long been silent and has departed with his family. We will not hear our tree pipit either, until next spring: he is busy feeding four large young in a nest nearby. Instead we have, as every year at this date, a newly arrived blackcap who will sing a few days then continue his post-breeding, gypsy life. Wall butterflies and blues are now common but meadow browns and gatekeepes are not yet flying. The peacocks and tortoiseshells of spring are all over: those of the second generation not yet come. When the sun comes out hot the horse-flies bite hotly too. And frequently it rains. In a word, it is high summer.

Honey still for Tea?

I am not noticeably an optimist except when it comes to bee-keeping. Every spring I stagger to my hives under a load of empty supers and place them hopefully on top. Then before putting the lid on I address encouraging words to the bees (for every good bee-keeper chats incessantly with his bees). 'Bees,' I say to them, 'once more I am providing you with a pile of empty boxes which, come the honey flow, I shall be greatly obliged if you will fill to overflowing. In return I will watch over you next winter and keep you safe from all the perils you would face in some precarious hollow tree. If famine threatens I will feed you on ample supplies of your own pure honey and will under no circumstances substitute harmful sugars such as are employed by many deceitful bee-masters.' So saying I shut the lid and leave the rest to nature, for I belong to the non-interfering school of bee-keepers. Now, near the end of July, it is time to reap the harvest if any. Soon I shall know the worst or the best. And if there is no honey I shall blame the weather or insecticides or the atom bomb: anything except the bees. For no experienced bee-man dares to speak ill of his bees. He knows that if he does they will certainly find some way of getting back at him.

Salute to a Country Diarist

It is comforting to know in so changing a world that some good things endure. When I became a *Guardian* reader ever so many years ago my favourite contributor of Country Diary pieces signed himself A.W.B. (in those days country diarists didn't have names, otherwise we would have known him as Arnold Boyd). Most of his notes were about the part of

Cheshire where he lived, but frequently he came into Wales where one of his favourite spots was a roadside pool near Newborough in Anglesey. That this large shallow pool eventually became a Mecca for bird-watchers was mainly because of his notes in the *Guardian*. Singularly rich in invertebrate life, the pool attracted large numbers of wading birds at times of migration and his accounts of the birds he saw there made exciting reading. But shallow pools have a way of getting shallower and eventually drying up altogether. So when I found myself in Anglesey last weekend for the first time for some years I almost didn't bother to visit the Newborough pool, thinking that by now it must have deteriorated. But not at all. Though the weather was appalling, I found a few people bird-watching there from their cars. I had just missed an avocet, they told me. But this didn't really matter amid the wealth of other waders that were present, many still in their spring plumage. It was, in fact, exactly the scene A.W.B. used to describe so well.

A Sacred Stream in Wales

Some rivers have definite sources but I can't think that anyone could claim to have discovered exactly where the Welsh river Dee rises. Looking for it the other day I followed the stream back till it was only a foot across but then found that it originates nowhere in particular. Instead, it comes oozing out of a wide peatbog along a hundred tiny channels. Or you could say it really springs out of the black cliffs of the mountain above. No matter, it's a good quiet spot reached only after a long uphill plod with no path to help you as you stumble over the tussocks of purple moorgrass.

In an earlier, simpler age than ours when rivers were gods, the Dee was the sacred stream of north Wales. But, mercifully, the Welsh have not perpetuated this tradition. Otherwise we would probably now have some crackpot shrine erected at the head of the river like the one the French set up last century at the source of the Seine showing a statue of a water nymph reclining in a fake grotto behind an iron railing with a souvenir shanty nearby. Instead, the source of the Dee remains entirely natural, or as natural as the ever-nibbling sheep allow any place to be, a place of heather, cotton-grass and reindeer moss and the wild moorland stretching round for miles. Long may it so remain.

Buzzards and Gamekeepers

Buzzards are long at their nesting. It was back in March when I noticed a pair going daily into the trees near my house. For hours they circled beautifully on their splendid broad wings and wailed to each other in excitement as they dived and climbed all over the sky in courtship fervour. By mid-April they had a big nest in the upper branches and at the end of the month I could see the female sitting. Now in July I go to pay my respects to the new generation. For the young are tall and brown-feathered and glare down at me with fierce eyes. I examine the ground at the foot of the tree for it usually has plenty to say about the buzzard's diet. Then I find myself wishing that I could have with me a party of those English gamekeepers who still destroy every buzzard they can. For I could show them the remains of all the crows and magpies, rats and mice that buzzards habitually feed their young on. To anyone who is not a gamekeeper it is easy to show that the countryside needs more hawks, not less, if it is to have a healthily balanced community of wild creatures. But how many gamekeepers or the shooting syndicates that pay them care about balanced communities of wild creatures? All most of them seem to want is a countryside infested with half-tame pheasants.

The Smallest Parish?

Happening to be in Chepstow this week I seized the opportunity of visiting the Wyndcliff. From that famous viewpoint I took the almost obligatory photograph of the Wye and then it occurred to me that it would be good to photograph the Wyndcliff itself from the opposite bank. So back I went to Chepstow and up the Gloucestershire side of the river. And that is how I came to Lancaut. It would be worth going to Lancaut, which a local woman told me was the smallest parish in all the world, just to see the tiny church, a roofless, plant-covered ruin down by the sluggish brown water of the tidal Wye where it goes round one of its hairpin bends between limestone cliffs. It was within one of these loops that the old parish of Lancaut was enclosed. It is a place, I would guess, of some prehistory as well as history. For this fertile, river-encircled spot looked a good defensible position to somebody (was it Iron Age man?) who built an earthwork across the narrow neck from river bend to river bend, thus cutting off Lancaut from the world. The old enclave retains something of its isolation even today, especially the church which is reached down a path through woodland bright with wild flowers of the limestone and full of wild broad-leaved trees that are such a relief after all the conifers of Tintern Forest.

The Romance (?) of Industry

I left my car by a river in one of those splendid tree-shaded picnic places the Forestry Commission has provided in so many choice spots. The sun was shining, the stream was full and fast and everything was just right for getting a photograph of the nearby waterfalls. All the same I never got there because as I went up the woodland trail I caught up with a man whose conversation was all about gold and who was bubbling over with the history of the local mine. So as I had never seen this particular gold-mine I decided to give the falls a miss and go with him along a path that lifted us steadily through the woods until we came up to a high bleak rocky mountainside. Little is now left of the old mine, just a few fern-covered walls, some flooded entrances, dangerous shafts and the usual ugly vomits of worthless rock. I could only think how appalling it must have been to have to work up there, especially in winter. My companion, however, was so excited by all the romance of industrial archaeology that he clearly did not share my gloomy thoughts. But my moment of happiness came later. On our way back we passed an old stone barn on whose door was a notice. 'This roof is used by bats which are protected by law. Do not disturb.' I suddenly felt glad to be living at a time when men no longer have to mine for gold up on that mountain in dreadful conditions for desperately low wages. And when we have broad enough margins to our lives to be able to worry about the survival of bats.

Spring in High Places

Now it is springtime. Or it was on Tuesday when a friend and I went scrambling up wet rocks and gullies within sight of Snowdon. It is one of the joys of mountains that in July, when the spring flowers of the lowlands have dried up in brownness and seed, you have to go only a couple of thousand feet above the valleys to find the year still new. So for us on Tuesday, as we followed a mountain stream back to its source, we also made our way back through June and May into April. On the highest ledge we reached, we found the finest show of flowers: a sheet of freshly opened bluebells among a yellow splendour of globe flowers and Welsh poppies. With these and many other lowland plants there were the true uplanders. The mountain sorrel was in full and splendid flower and with it the white stars of the mossy saxifrage. The rock walls, those in damp places, were patched bright-green with alpine ferns and we managed to find a beautiful specimen of the holly fern, now so uncommon in Wales. Among the flowering plants our rarest find was the alpine cinquefoil which was just beginning to open its yellow five-petalled flowers. But it is not the rarities that are the chief delight of looking for plants on mountains. What is most wonderful is the unfailing luxuriance of all the many species that crowd together on these most elevated and fertile places. For even in those summers when the lowlands are gasping with heat and sunburn, the upland terraces keep their coolness and moisture because they have a climate of their own.

Snowdon's Old Herbalists

On Monday a party of us clambered slowly up the eastern flank of Snowdon to look for alpine plants. The day was hot and we were grateful for the mists that wrapped around us from time to time. One of the pleasures of seeking Snowdon's plants is that they have a distinguished place in history as the first British mountain plants to be recorded in any numbers. A list of them was made in 1639 by Thomas Johnson, a London apothecary deeply learned in the uses of plants. He is an interesting figure in the annals, straddling the dividing line between old-world herbalism and the emerging science of botany. Although it was high summer when Johnson climbed Snowdon, the whole mountain remained buried in cloud all day and he and his friends would surely have got lost in the mists if they had not 'obtained the services of a country boy as guide'. There has always been something of a mystery about Johnson's visit. Snowdon is a big, sprawling mountain whose botanically exciting localities are so few that a stranger could easily spend a day up there and miss all the choicest spots. But we know from his list that Johnson did really well and must have got to the most rewarding places. So how did he manage it? I can't help thinking that although the credit for the discovery of these alpines is given to Johnson and other English visitors, they had probably been known to the local Welsh herbalists for ages but had never been placed on record. I wish we knew more about that 'country boy' who acted as Johnson's guide. Perhaps he had already learned more about mountain plants than Johnson ever was to know.

Polecats are sometimes red

I had a moment of excitement the other day when I half glimpsed a reddish-brown furry animal moving through the bracken. Normally a creature of that colour would have to be a stoat but this one was too big for any stoat, and I was immediately convinced I had seen a mammal I have been hoping for all my life, the rare pine marten. The marten, formerly widespread in Britain, has long been known to survive in and around Snowdonia and a recent survey confirms it is still here, though in very small numbers. When I saw my supposed pine marten I stood still, my back against a tree, in case it might reappear. Sure enough it soon came circling back, as I could see by the moving of the bracken stems, and then it broke cover and came hunting, nose down, across a patch of short turf and I got a perfect view of it as it passed within six feet of me without having the slightest suspicion of my presence. I could then see that this was no marten but a red variety of the polecat whose normal colour is black. Perhaps I ought to have guessed this at the start, but it is many years since I have seen or heard of the red polecats which used to be quite common in this district, and I had long ago assumed they had died out. But though I was fooled this time I'm sure I will go on hoping to meet up with a genuine marten some day.

A Plea for Ants

Most gardeners are not in love with insects. They tolerate bees and butterflies and throw insecticides at the rest. Ants are among the commonest insects in our garden. But are they pests or not? Some gardeners swear they are. Investigating rock plants which looked miserable, they have found ants' nests disturbing the roots and perhaps poisoning them with formic acid. All the same my guess is that on balance the multitudinous presence of ants in our garden is as beneficial as earthworms or falling leaves. What moves me to the defence of ants just now is something I saw this morning. I was looking out of the window when a lovely female green woodpecker flew down to the lawn closely followed by a young one. Mother woodpecker went straight to an ants' nest, filled her beak with ants with astonishing speed and then shovelled the whole lot into her infant's gaping mouth. It was a charming scene which would not have been possible in a garden where ants are destroyed. There'll be a similar happening next month when the flying ants come out and rise heavenwards in their thousands. Mysteriously appearing from nowhere, the black-headed gulls will circle silently and gracefully about the sky, skilfully snapping up these tasty insects. But I fear my entomological friends will rebuke me for being so enthusiastic about the death of so many ants. Quite properly they could point out that most wonderful of all are the ants themselves and their social organisation worked out millions of years ago and still superior to anything man has yet devised.

A Peatbog Treasure

For the past few years a team of enthusiasts has been carrying out a survey of the wild plants of Montgomeryshire and eventually their records will be published in what promises to be a very interesting volume. Among the rarer species in the county is a tiny insect-eating plant called the intermediate sundew. Previous records showed that this sundew had been reported only once in the county and that was in a peatbog not far from here about thirty years ago. And since I was the one who then found it, there was clearly some obligation on my part to go and see if it was still there. For I had to confess that in all that time I had never been back to check on it. So last Tuesday I dutifully went off bog-trotting though with little hope of remembering the exact spot or that the plant would still be there. For about two hours I searched rather despairingly without seeing even the round-leaved sundew which is locally common in this district but just as I was about to give up I came to where the peatbog ended at the edge of a wood. Then in the curious way in which the memory sometimes works, everything seemed to click into place and I felt sure I had reached the right spot. Sure enough I went only a few more paces and there was my sundew. So I went on my way rejoicing that after thirty years not only this little plant but a whole peatbog was still intact. But I wonder for how much longer in these drainage-mad, peat-hungry days?

AUGUST

Know Coriander by its Smell?

This year in the garden we have a beautiful pinkish-white umbellifer called coriander. Because when growing wild in Britain it is always near houses it is evidently an alien, presumably introduced from the Levant where it is undoubtedly native. But it is a plant with a long history in Britain for its remains have been identified at a Bronze Age hut-site in Kent. One wonders whether it grew naturally in Britain in the warmer Bronze Age climate or whether it came here from the east Mediterranean with the migrations of prehistoric man. Probably it was a deliberate introduction for it is an anciently esteemed herb with uses ranging from the treatment of flatulence to the flavouring of sweets.

A curious aspect of coriander emerges if we consult *The Flora of the British Isles* by Clapham, Tutin and Warburg. Here we are solemnly (?) assured that '*the whole plant smells strongly of bed-bugs*'. But so what? Could it be that this fascinating information sheds more light on botanists than on botany? One is tempted to conclude that before they rose to professional dignity the learned authors of our *Flora* languished in such unhygienic squalor that they learned only too well what bed-bugs smell like. But how many of their readers will be similarly informed? Would you, gently nurtured *Guardian* reader, know a bed-bug by its smell? If not, I fear you may not recognise coriander if you find it.

Budding Naturalists, 1970

One of the saddest things about adults is that the majority have lost their childhood curiosity about the natural world. Thus the other day as I wandered past a river-bank picnic spot I found inevitably that of eight people present the four adults were sitting in their cars. But their four little children were paddling in the stream very happily because they had discovered that by turning over the stones they could find the little fish called bullheads lying under them. Suddenly one of them cried out with special excitement. He had caught something different. But what was it? He raced with it to his father in the nearby car. But father, communing with the mysteries of his Sunday paper, was not a bit interested. I asked to see the little fish squirming in the child's cupped hands and was surprised to find it was a stone loach, a species

I had not suspected to exist in that particular stream. So here was infant curiosity making its contribution to natural history. The lesson is self-apparent. Before these kids grow up into adults who find nature rather a bore unless fed to them on the telly, their enthusiasm could be channelled. I hear there is a scheme at present to map the distribution of our fish. Why not organise the toddlers to survey the bullhead and the stone loach? Would any age-group go at it with greater zeal?

Ring Out Wild Bells, 1961

A few days ago I did the ridge-walk of Pumlumon: that is to say I did one of the finest ridge-walks in all Wales. I started in the north in Montgomeryshire, going by Glaslyn, a shining, circular, plantless, stony-margined lake set high in a purple heather moor. Then down to a long, water-lily lake called Bugeilyn, which means the Shepherd's Lake. But no shepherds live thereabouts now. Only hydo-electricians and their inevitable retinue of Irishmen. Not that there is anything new about Irishmen in the Welsh hills. They were here already in prehistoric times and maybe it was Irish fingers that dropped the little flint arrowheads found in the bog by Bugeilyn; and Irish hands that raised the once great cairns on Pumlumon.

If so I hope they enjoyed Pumlumon as much as I did: the views across Wales; the untramelled, undulating miles of the high plateau; the mountain silence; the coolness of the uplands after the airless, hot valleys.

It was in a spirit of exhilaration that I came swiftly down the final great slopes to Nant-y-moch. After that who better to give me a lift back to civilisation than one whose joy it is to ring bells? To ring out the bells seemed a fitting end to such a day. So two hours after leaving Pumlumon's summit cairn I was watching a bob major being rung in the great square tower of the church of Llanbadarn Fawr near Aberystwyth.

Inside a Mountain of Slate

One day last week I really went to earth, reaching a mile underground, not downwards but horizontally. For that is often the way with mines and quarries in hilly country: you follow a perfectly level road straight into the centre of a mountain. After that it may wind up to higher levels or down to lower ones until you realise that the whole interior of the mountain is penetrated by tunnels and hollowed here and there into vast halls. That robust old expression, the bowels of the earth, perfectly describes a slate mine, with wagon trains of rock passing through the intestines like digested food.

There was the strange experience of walking in silence through all that rock and then rounding a bend to see moving lights and find men working in a dimly lit cavern: men with lamps on their foreheads hammering and drilling, or carefully tapping sticks of gelignite into holes and exploding them without ceremony or even much noise. It seems all unspeakably dangerous but everybody's nonchalance reassures you.

All our values are relative. When I went into the mine it was a miserable, cold, wet afternoon. When I came out an hour later the weather was exactly the same. But after the darkness and chill of the mine, the world outside, for all the rain, was bright, colourful and deliciously warm. So it is worth going into a mine if only for the joy of coming out of one.

Lord Knows how to Spot a Bog Orchid

When the Lord had made our British orchids I think he found he had a bit of the vital essence left over and wondered what to do with it. I reckon he looked at his distribution maps and realised he'd overdone it a bit in places on the chalk and limestone. So he sat and thought deep ecological thoughts about all those acid moors and bogs in the north and west where there were miles of heather and cotton-grass but scarcely an orchid in sight. More and more he regretted spending so much time in Kent, but what to do?

Gloomily he looked at his empty paint-box and wept for all those wonderful colours he had lavished on spider orchids, helleborines and lady's slippers from the south of England to Yorkshire. Now all he had left was the meagrest pinch of green stuff. Sadly he fashioned it into a sort of orchid, smaller and more miserable than any orchid in creation, and just plain green all over. He had to plant it in bogs on top of the moss, for anywhere else it would have been choked by the flimsiest grasses. And there it still grows, rather rare and hard to find.

I saw it there last week only because I was shown it. Still, I daresay even the

Lord is pretty pleased with himself when he manages to find a bog orchid, wretched though it is.

Ferns along the Wayside

Going down the wood path to post a letter I consoled myself for the trickle of water down my neck with the thought that if it were not for our wet climate the Welsh valleys would be less rich in ferns. On the way back I counted how many species I could find between the village and home. In a bank by the main road were hart's-tongue, soft shield-fern and black spleenwort. A mortared wall yielded rusty-back, wall-rue and common spleenwort. Then the road passes under trees and immediately there was a wealth of lady fern, sweet mountain fern, common buckler-fern and two kinds of male fern. After a clearing in the woods which gave me only bracken, the path drops steeply into a gorge-like valley where polypodies bristle from the branches and beech-ferns adorn the damp rocks. A wet bank provided my last species, the hard fern, making a total of fifteen, which seems a satisfactory tally to get in the space of one mile and without deviating an inch from the road.

Without going more than another mile I could have added five more. In the shadiest, wettest part of the gorge I would have seen hay-scented buckler-fern on the river bank with both the filmy-ferns. My nineteenth kind would have been parsley-fern on the rocks above the gorge and my twentieth, moonwort in a nearby pasture.

After the Woodmen, the Flowers

It is eighteen months since the tree-fellers came to our local wood. The affair was soon over. Down went the thin oaks and birches. Great fires ate up the brushwood. There was a planting of conifers and beeches. The sheep were fenced out for the first time for ages. Next summer there was a noticeable increase in the ground flora but nothing very remarkable. It is this second summer that has produced wonders. First there was the yellow archangel. This had never been anything better than a struggler here, existing only in cracks of wet rocks beyond the reach of sheep. But by this spring it had come down off the rocks and made a wide yellow patch on the flat floor of the wood along with a riotous increase of primroses, herb Robert and upright St. John's wort.

Then came the foxgloves. Where there used to be hardly any, acres of wood now glowed with them. They have been followed by an unprecedented eruption of meadow-sweet, enchanter's nightshade and angelica. So now we enjoy the strange experience of wading through waist-deep vegetation where we used to pass through the trees on a pasture-like sward. But I am forgetting the grasses of many kinds. They have leapt towards the light and spread joyously far and wide; none more exuberant, graceful or colourful than the tall, silvery-purple tufts of the wavy hair-grass.

Caterpillar Problems

When I want to identify a caterpillar I have two books to consult. One is modern and in English, the other is old and in French. I try the English one first. Laboriously I pore over the descriptions and the dingy illustrations that make most caterpillars look alike. But if I do not find my caterpillar there I know I am lost, for I can never find it in the French book. Not that this book is uninformative or out of date (though it was published in 1832). It is just that the illustrations are so perfect.

In spite of the lapse of 130 years the caterpillars they depict lie on the page like living caterpillars, still so brilliantly gleaming in their greens, golds and browns, every hair, bristle and spot so clear and sharp that you expect the creatures to go looping or wriggling off the page and away across the table.

Looking at them I become entranced. I turn over and there is another remarkable plate and more and more after that, eventually leading me away from British species altogether to the exotics of the Midi, bizarrely tufted beauties in bright yellows and blues. Then there are all the chrysalids to look at and they are stranger still: slender, dumpy, sombre, brilliant, smooth or grotesquely warty. I end in a dream of the splendours of the south of France. It is all very wonderful. But it does not identify my caterpillar.

The Moorland Heart of Wales, 1958

Recently I walked to the top of Pumlumon. After the rains of August the track up to the old mine from Eisteddfa Gurig had become a stream. Still it provided the only firm going in a land entirely splash and squelch. Above the mine I left the track in the hope of finding a drier route to the top. Instead, the way got spongier with every yard until I found myself floundering across a wilderness of rushes and sphagnum moss where water flowed over my feet wherever I went. But at last I came up quite suddenly to a short, springy turf and then to a wide stony terrain where there was little vegetation of any sort: the zone of the club-mosses.

In a few minutes I was looking round from the top. To the south I could see right across the remarkable plateau that is the moorland heart of Wales, ridge beyond straight blue ridge, smoothed and planed to one level in the ancientness of time. My view to the north was barred by a fathoms-deep indigo cloud that lay right across from Cader Idris to Aran Fawddwy, as if all Meirionnydd were engulfed in one great storm. But about me the sun shone softly on the rocks of the summit cairn. The air was breathlessly still and everywhere lay the silence peculiar to mountains, broken only by the occasional owk-owk-owk of ravens barking far away.

An Ancient Way Over Berwyn, 1960

Lately, in search of ancient things, I was in the fair vale of Edeirnion along the River Dee, a district that needs no praise from anyone. To see across all this fine country you need a high viewpoint such as you can find anywhere along the upper flanks of Berwyn. Take Ffordd Gam Elin, for instance, the very old road which leaves B4401 a mile north-east of Llandrillo and climbs steeply and full of purpose away to the south-east. At first it is a tarmac road but at last becomes a green road through heather moor, getting fainter as it goes up and away round the curves of the hills. But maybe you do not wish to go with it very far but prefer to diverge to the hill-top you see on the north-east side of the road (map reference SJ 056372). If so you will come not only up to a viewpoint but also to a perfect Bronze Age circle. On the flat summit stand forty-one stones, the tallest about thirty inches, set close together in a ring twelve yards across, with an entrance south-west and, in the centre, the hollow of an opened grave. A strange, atmosphered place this, a place to go up to on a fine, calm, moonlit, curlew-wailing, snipe-bleating night to think about remotely past men, the dark interiors of their minds (and yours?) and of the magic they ascribed to circles.

Hairstreaks in the Oak Tops

The other day I sat on a hill above the estuary, bird-watching the idle way instead of going down to the mudflats and making an honest effort to find birds. I got what I deserved—no birds of any great interest. But unexpectedly I found I was on a good perch for butterfly-watching. From my rocky ridge I had perfect views of the handsome little butterfly called the purple hairstreak. This is a species that is far from rare but normally is seldom observed because it hardly ever visits flowers, preferring to fly always within a few feet of the higher branches of oaks. It chanced that my perch was surrounded by little oaks stunted by the estuary winds and all growing below me down steep banks. I was therefore on a level with the crowns of some of these trees and the purple hairstreaks were easily visible every time they fluttered up out of the leaves and quickly settled again. Through binoculars I could clearly see the brilliant flash of dark-purple on their open wings. There is another hairstreak that is far less common and which I have never yet seen, though it is recorded from this district. It is the brown hairstreak. And since it flies in August and September it is something to look out for right now. So maybe the next time I am lazy about bird-watching will be my brown hairstreak day. Ever optimistic us naturalists.

George Borrow's Favourite Mountain

On Wednesday I went off to climb what to me is the greatest of the lesser mountains of north Wales. It is the one that fills the skyline when you look north from Llyn Tegid (Bala Lake) and its name is Arennig. It is only 2,800ft but because it is set apart from other ranges, it stands prominent in the view from many far-off places. From the south and west, it appears tall and shapely, its flanks rough with tumbles of loose stones. But in the north and east, it raises great crags that give it true mountain qualities. So much so that George Borrow, who knew a proper mountain when he saw one, wrote of it: 'Of all the hills that I saw in Wales, none made a greater impression on me'. It was from the north that I set out, finding no tracks except those made by sheep. For the paths on the less popular mountains are often more imagined than real, no matter how convincing they look on a map. Up and up I scrambled through heather and rocks. Above a lake I found a gully which somehow found a way up between the cliffs and so to the summit. For once, I was lucky with the weather. The clouds of early morning had miraculously blown away and bright sunshine gleamed on grass and rock. The southward prospect was immense across central Wales. But the hoped for view of Snowdon was lost as the next surge of clouds rolled in from the sea; and not for the first time this year I had to scuttle ignominiously down a mountain to escape a deluge.

Know a Swallow when you see one?

Can you tell a swallow from a house martin? Until today I have always thought it easy. A swallow has a long tail and its back is all black, while a martin has a short tail and its back is black but with a conspicuous white rump. But this morning this distinction broke down completely as I watched a bird flying round for over an hour without my being able to say whether it was a martin or a young swallow which had not yet grown its tail. My difficulty sprang from very unusual circumstances: every feather of this bird was pure white. It was an eye-catching sight as it flew back and forth and people in the nearby houses were sure that it first appeared only yesterday. Without hesitation they called it a martin because there are martins' nests on their houses. But they may not be right, for the farm building nearby has a colony of swallows and it was their company that the white bird seemed to me to be favouring. The books tell us that most kinds of birds have been known to produce complete albinos but how many do we ever see? I have never met with one before except once long ago, a starling. Albino birds are said to have a poor chance of survival either because they are constitutionally weak or because their white plumage singles them out for attacks by hawks. And now swallows and martins alike will soon be off on far migrations that will tax both their strength and their ability to get away from hawks. So, whether it be swallow or martin, I do not expect to see our little albino coming back next spring.

Full House in the Heronry

This year there has been an impressive increase in our local heronry. Counting their tree-top nests in May we found a gain of sixty per cent over last year. By mid-June young herons were daily pouring out of the trees to make their maiden flights down the estuary. And now the last ones are about to go. As we pass by we see them standing tall on long legs that look so awkward for tree-top life. They take little heed of us. Instead they gaze away to the distant hills as if lost in thought. Through a telescope we can bring them very close, and can look right into their strange staring eyes, and ask ourselves what sort of thought goes on in the brain behind. Presumably very little. Herons, I dare say, are still chewing over thoughts that first struck them in the Pleistocene age. Not that they are the worse off for that. By some freak of evolution man may have succeeded in thinking a few new thoughts since the Pleistocene, but is he or the world any better off because of it? Herons may not have much brain in their thin heads but at least their life is totally sane and robust. They may increase now and then but it is never for long. The next hard winter will cut them down to size and there is no danger they can ever infest the earth. A pity we cannot make the same claim for ourselves.

Sparrowhawks at Home

It was in late spring we noticed the sparrowhawk's nest high up in a larch close to our path homeward through the wood. From then on, though we passed that way daily, it was rare that the sitting bird or her mate gave the slightest sign of being aware of our passing, though they must have seen or heard us every time. Even when the four young were a month old, and standing tall on the nest, that part of the wood was always silent except when the parent hawks brought food and the young squealed in excitement. A week later all were in the nearby tree-tops. Any day now, we said, they will be gone. But we were wrong. They grew strong on the wing and could fly round and over the wood like arrows but still they remained attached to the place. They became noisier every day, mewing like kittens, but much more loudly, keeping it up with few intervals all day long. And now, though it is mid-August, they are still there, wailing in the larch tops so that their parents can always find them as soon as they arrive with prey. As I write this in my garden half a mile away I can hear their clear calling on the still morning air. A sound to delight most bird-watchers but to make gamekeepers grow pale.

Favourite Welsh Viewpoints

I am very grateful to all the kind folk who let me know about their favourite Welsh viewpoints and I only regret I cannot answer them individually. Thanks to them I now know quite a lot about other people's ideas of scenery. Not everyone, for instance, wants fair weather. One Welsh typewriter obviously shook with emotion as it tried to do justice to Snowdon swirled round by Wagnerian clouds and thunderous rain. The hour immediately after rain was kind to another correspondent who reached Y Drum high above Llanfairfechan and saw all Anglesey, most of Snowdonia and north-east Wales, the coast from Great Orme to Southport, the tower of Blackpool (through binoculars) and the dark profile of the Peak in Derbyshire. The majority of favourite north Wales scenes included Snowdon somewhere in the picture but the viewpoints, mostly distant, ranged from Anglesey all round the south to near Oswestry. A highly-recommended viewpoint closer to Snowdon was Dyniewyd, a hill east of Beddgelert. Llŷn, Yr Eifl (the Rivals) and the Meirionnydd hills and estuaries were almost as popular as Snowdon. One original soul turned his back and looked across to Ireland from the end of Llŷn. And an enthusiast with an advertiser's cunning tried to persuade me that the genuinely best views were only to be had from trains on the Tal-y-llyn railway! Of course there was plenty of support for mid-Wales and the south. But these I must leave till next week.

More Cherished Panoramas

To conclude our catalogue of readers' favourite Welsh viewpoints. Outside of Snowdonia support came for the quiet beauty of the Vyrnwy valley at Meifod; the Severn valley around Newtown; and the middle Wye at Builth. South-west of Builth we are offered a hill called The Begwns which gives a '360 degrees viewpoint of splendid scenery including Brecon Beacons and Black Mountains'. It is these two fine ranges, as seen from various angles, that get most of the south Wales support. One reader recommends the view not to but from the Black Mountains looking north over Hay-on-Wye into central Wales. Glamorgan evidently has a great viewpoint on Mynydd Caerau a few miles north of Bridgend: from there a reader saw much of south Wales from Presely to Sugar Loaf and a vast sweep of Somerset and Devon. Not surprisingly someone speaks up for Gwent's Wyndcliff, famous for centuries for its remarkable panorama of the Wye gorge above Chepstow as well as the country east and west and far into Somerset.

Snakes do not always retreat

This seems to be a good year for snakes. In the marshy ground outside my garden I have seen only an occasional snake in the past fifteen years. Yet this spring I see one nearly every time I go out. Some are grass snakes, long and thin and of lovely pastel shades of green or brown. But most are adders, and these are shorter, thicker, darker and looking every inch the venomous creatures they are. Not that they are usually aggressive, these adders. As soon as they feel the first tremor of the ground under your footsteps they usually swish into the rushes and you never see them again. In fact, I have always believed that adders are never hostile to people unless injured by them. But today I made an adder very cross by unintentionally getting between him and his lair. How was I to know that he was lying out in the sun ten yards from home instead of his usual ten feet? When he felt the earth tremble as I approached, he began to race for cover only to find me right in his path. But such is the pride and self-confidence of adders that he didn't hesitate an instant. Instead he raised his little head several inches off the ground and, hissing in a most alarming manner, came straight towards me as if he assumed I would get smartly out of his way. In this I did not disappoint him.

Access to the Uplands? 1970

Let me tell you about two friends of mine. One is a Welsh farmer. From his isolated home in the hills of mid-Wales he looks at magnificent scenery all round; there is peace and always the air is pure. He loves the hills and he loathes the idea of a Cambrian Mountains National Park. He runs a car made in Birmingham. My other friend lives on a Midlands housing estate. He is not happy there—too many neighbours, too much traffic, not a trace of beauty in the scene. He slaves nightly in a car factory. At heart he too is a countryman and while he works his thoughts are often in the hills of Wales where he loves to go at weekends. His income is probably about the same as my Welsh farming friend. In earning these wages he occupies only a few square yards of space. But my farming friend requires 2,000 acres to earn the same amount and then only with the support of heavy subsidies. So the question naturally arises: can he really expect to go on occupying all that mountain land and go on keeping all those Midlanders at bay? I'm afraid he is increasingly an anomaly, this man who thinks he has the right to enjoy the cars the Midlanders make but not the company of the Midlanders themselves. But he will find they are not a bad lot when he gets to know them.

Cowries' Ancient Appeal

We may no longer choose to clutter our houses with cases of butterflies, birds' eggs and bric-à-brac as middle-class Victorians used to do; but still the collecting urge keeps its hold on us. Any fine day on our local beach you can see holidaymakers bent earnestly searching for shells to take home as souvenirs. Most are content to find just any kind of shell. A more discerning minority like to know a little about what they find and they carry field guides to help them to give names to the various topshells, periwinkles and whelks. No doubt one thing all these collectors have in common is an instinctive appreciation of the shape and pattern of shells. One day I asked some children who seemed to be searching with special intentness whether they were looking for some particular shell. They were indeed. Their particular quest was for cowries, they said very knowingly. What they did not know was that in falling for the fascination of cowries they were probably throwing back to something very ancient in the human mind. Man seems always to have made a cult of shells; and cowries have had a special place in this cult. They have been widely used as money: and it is also thought that cowries may have been objects of very powerful symbolism. How fascinating then to find modern city children thus unconsciously making a direct contact with such primitive values.

Passing of an All-round Naturalist, 1980

With sadness we heard this week of the death of one of the most esteemed of Welsh naturalists, Tommie Warren Davis, who lived near the shores of Milford Haven. He was one of those rare people who manage to approach nature on a broad front, yet still succeed in being specialists in certain fields. So you could not only take him a caterpillar, a moth, a grasshopper, a beetle or a wild flower and be perfectly confident he would be able to name it accurately; you could also ask him to identify one of those notoriously difficult dandelions, hawkweeds or brambles and he would probably give you a pretty good idea what it was. Yet meet him another time and you might get the impression that birds or maybe mammals were his real passion. He seemed to amble through his years of retirement in such a quiet and genial way that those not well-acquainted with him had no idea of how industrious he was or of what a major part he played in conservation. He will be remembered as a botanist, especially as the author of *Plants of Pembrokeshire* (1970), a publication of the West Wales Naturalists Trust. To the average amateur this work may seem the last possible word on the subject. To Warren Davis it was hardly more than a makeshift list compiled to help people for the time being, while he got on with his much greater project: a full-scale flora of Pembrokeshire. But as so often happens with ageing naturalists struggling to record the results of a lifetime of observation, his time ran out just too soon. Perhaps in one more year he would have completed what promised to be a marvellous piece of work. Now it is left to others, if they can be found, to conclude this formidable task.

Quiet Castles in Gwent

Castles are a curious enthusiasm. They are monuments to violence, tyranny and rapacity, yet we love them. So this week I have been doing the castles of Gwent. I suppose I was caught early by castles for one of my clearest infant memories is of looking up at Harlech castle and marvelling that in all the world there could be so many jackdaws. Since then I have learnt to connect castles with wildflowers as well as birds. For despite all that the Ministry of Works can do to give them an antiseptic look, castle walls persist in being miniature nature reserves.

Besides, castles are often in such good surroundings. So Grosmont, sited beautifully on its mound, looks to a delight of green hills along the Monnow river. Not far down-stream is Skenfrith, a castle that at first repels you by its bareness; yet all is forgiven when you see how well placed it is beside its lovely river. Water enhances all castles, as you find again at White Castle which has all that a castle should have: high walls, a deep flowery moat all round and a tower with a view of the whole district. Then not far off is Raglan, a great castle which outclasses these lesser forts. But to me Raglan is like Tintern Abbey: its beauty is sadly diminished by all those parked cars and by the main road roaring near. So give me the remoter, minor castles where visitors are fewer.

Moths of Summer Nights

Lately a friend had been using our garden as a site for his moth-catching trap. It is a lamp which sheds an eerie green light across the lawn at night and looks like something just arrived from outer space. At dusk, the moths come to it from all directions but once inside the dark interior of the trap they settle quietly and are harmlessly released next morning. What the trap has mostly caught are the common moths of August. But one little yellow beauty, called the vestal, was a visitor from southern Europe, just one of many insects which in a summer like this are quick to suppose that Britain is part of the Mediterranean region. It is sad that their hopes of getting established here are so very slight. A typical British winter followed by a typical British summer will put paid to them all. Perhaps many of these immigrants were residents here when our summers were always summery. Reading through old records we get glimpses of what a different world there was only a century or so ago. There are accounts, for instance, of a butterfly called the black-veined white which has long been extinct or nearly so in Britain. Yet if you had gone to Cardiff in April, 1858, you would have seen its caterpillars feeding in thousands on blackthorn bushes. Perhaps it was soon after then that our climate lost its continental flavour. Today, we can only be thankful that we still get the occasional summer when we can welcome the vestals and the clouded yellows, knowing that we will probably not be seeing them again for many a long year.

By Narrow-gauge to Ffestiniog

Although I have never been numbered amongst the ranks of the narrow-gauge railway enthusiasts, I did let them give me a whirl up their famous Ffestiniog line on Tuesday, and I greatly enjoyed it despite the weather. I also admired the dedication and friendliness of all these volunteers who so cheerfully give their time to this and similar amateur railways. And the power of those little engines! Hauling long trains packed with people fourteen miles up hill was no problem at all. Our engine was a fairly new machine, but even the most ancient locomotives sail up the line as if they were enjoying it as much as the passengers. Between the showers, the views across the vale were superb, and there were long stretches of steep woodland where we seemed to be flying through the tree-tops like birds. Then just before journey's end, there was a great moment when the line circled completely round and crossed over itself. It was better than Spaghetti Junction! The object of this neat manoeuvre is to lift the line up the hillside and so avoid a reservoir. From up there we got more splendid vistas and even when our upward journey ended in that dour slate town at the head of the vale, we still had those lovely stark mountains that rise sheer above the houses and make Blaenau Ffestiniog one of the dramatic towns of Britain. But we were not there for long. The whistle blew with a romantic sound and off we steamed to enjoy the trip all the way back down to the sea.

National Park Solitude

Wednesday being a rare bright day, I took myself off to the hills of south-eastern Snowdonia. The north-west wind was quite cold, but that is just what you want for an upland walk in summer. All along the north, the high peaks stood up with startling clarity and so did the moorlands of mid-Wales to the south. If only we were free to choose, this is the sort of day we would always wait for before venturing up the mountains: the day after the last depression, the day before the next. Even in the most dismal summers the sportive gods grant us a few scattered days of this perfect kind; blue with dazzling white clouds that sail endlessly across the sky yet bring scarcely any interruption of the sunshine. You can't walk far in this part of Snowdonia without being struck by how quiet it all is. Nearly all the National Park visitors make for the north and west where the famous mountains are, and the tracks are worn out by countless boots. But in the south-east, though this is also marvellous walking country, the paths are so little used that many are quite hard to find. So it was on Wednesday. I set off on a trail that started with a reassuring signpost but, well before I had reached 2,000 feet, I had nothing but my compass to guide me through the heather. I walked all day without seeing anyone at all, not even in the farthest distance. I suppose those who run the National Park would like to see a better balance of visitor pressure. But for lovers of solitude, things are perfect as they are.

What Price Progress?

The hot weather of last week defeated me. In the end I retreated indoors and picked a book at random from the shelf. Happily it was *The Natural History And Antiquities Of Selborne* by Gilbert White: is there a cooler, more refreshing book in the whole of English literature? Those who put a specially high value on the natural world can only be envious of the almost unchanging eighteenth-century scene that White inhabited. True, he notes somewhere that the deer were vanishing from the local forests. But apart from that, the notion that nature might need conserving was far from his everyday thoughts and he certainly never dreamed that the day would come when even common plants and animals would be threatened by human activities. But in the following century the idea of progress took the world by storm and was resisted only by a tiny few who, like Thoreau in America, could foresee that nature was about to be devastated. Today we no longer say much about progress. But it is still with us, only now we call it growth. However, I must not go on like this. As a country diarist I tend to get rebuked if I do anything other than 'babble of green fields', as Shakespeare put it. Yet even green fields can be a troublesome subject. Not the old herb-rich meadows of Gilbert White's day but our modern pastures, the product of scientific agriculture. Despite many honest efforts to reconcile farming with wildlife, most farmers still seem terrified by the sight of a few wildflowers and their 'improved' fields remain as vividly and unnaturally green as ever.

The Shelducks' Farewell

Now is the time when our river says farewell to one of its most splendid birds, those large and colourful shelducks which for many months have been our constant neighbours. Every morning from April to June they came flying from the sandy wastes of the estuary to circle over the fields. Then, if all was clear, they fluttered down to hold their parliaments in the nearby woods where they made their downy nests in old rabbit burrows. When the ducklings hatched they were led by their parents at dawn on a long march to the estuary where the rich food supplies are renewed at every tide. By early July the young were nearly full grown and becoming independent, a signal that the moment had come for the adults to go off on their long holiday off the coast of Germany. Such shore-loving ducks, you might suppose, must be very reluctant to take the direct overland route to Germany. Yet that is the way they go. This mustering of the shelduck clans beyond the North Sea is a strange affair and only the shelducks really know why they do it. All we can say is that they gather there in their tens of thousands and go through a thorough moulting before they come back home near the end of the year. It would be lovely to see them passing over on these migrations but unfortunately they travel mostly by night. Only very rarely have I seen groups of them taking off from here in the dusk of late summer and heading eastwards into the darkness of the hills. Presumably they do not come down again until they reach the German shore.

SEPTEMBER

Fear of Spiders Inborn?

Further to my remarks about people's fear of small creatures, a Liverpool reader reports that he has heard that people who dread mice have no fear of spiders, and vice versa. He says that although both he and his daughter are antipathetic to spiders they have no fear of mice; but his wife, who has no fear of spiders, cannot bear mice. He also makes the point that, regretfully aware of his own spider-fear, he made every effort to prevent his daughter from acquiring it. So although spiders sent shudders up and down his spine he bravely used to invite his infant daughter to inspect spiders and their webs with him, and to use his words, 'never did I let her see that I disliked the creatures'.

But in spite of these precautions, at about three years old the child suddenly showed fear of spiders, a fear she has retained ever since although she is now grown up and is a biologist. Therefore my correspondent concludes that there must be something innate in these phobias and that I was wrong last week in suggesting that they are mainly acquired by children imitating their parents. He also doubts if the correct teaching of nature study could have much effect on these phobias. Knowledge and appreciation of the beauty of spiders' webs, he says, have done nothing to eliminate the horror of spiders either for himself or his daughter. A sad conclusion this, if it is a true one.

History amongst the Mine-shafts

If I were asked to take a foreign visitor to some place in Wales where he could get a really vivid glimpse into the past I doubt if I would take him to any of our historical monuments. Far too often such monuments manage to leave the imagination cold. They are somehow not human enough. I would prefer to show a visitor something quite humble and workaday, some token of the lives and labours, continuous over a long period of time, of ordinary man.

So I would let him see a lead-mine in a valley in upland Cardiganshire where you can take in 2,000 years of human toil at a glance. For here the ruins of modern mines lie side by side with workings that probably date back to pre-Roman days.

The old walls, the bits of abandoned machinery and the grey vomit of spoil from these gaping mines evoke the toil, sweat and life of past ages far more intimately than any castle, tomb or temple. Here is an ancient monument that shows you twenty centuries of human vitality and which no Office of Works has sterilised. Search round on the spoil heaps and you will soon be picking up querns—hollowed stone blocks in which ore was pounded—and which were last held in human fingers perhaps five centuries ago. Or if you climb high up the hillside you can see quantities of stone hammers that have been lying there ever since they were broken and discarded in early Celtic times.

Revelations in the Drought, 1959

I hope that all parish historians (may their tribe increase) have taken full advantage of the recent drought. I mean I hope they have carefully recorded the results of all the great labours undertaken by the hundreds of countryfolk who this summer have had to turn themselves into archaeologists and seek out old springs and forgotten wells. Not for a long time can there have been such questioning of aged villagers, such ransacking of old memories, such unearthing of local history.

I saw a good example of such discoveries on Bardsey Island, north Wales. A damp spot on a hillside was dug into for water and the removal of a great amount of rocks and earth revealed a small, square, stone-lined well (full of water) which could possibly have been the original water supply of Bardsey Abbey, the ruins of which lie nearby. It is remarkable that such a fine well could have been lost sight of and that not a memory seems to have survived of it. And how happens it that what is possibly the island's most dependable well was so deeply buried? Was it the slow debris of the years that filled it? Or was it the victim of anti-papist feeling at the Dissolution because it was a holy well? Whatever the truth, if something as vital as a well can be lost on so small an island, it makes you wonder what a wealth of other past things await discovery there and elsewhere.

In those days they could Walk

Some interesting letters have survived written by a young gentlewoman who in July, 1787, went with her father on a daring holiday jaunt from Birmingham to Aberystwyth. For over half the way there was a post-chaise service by way of Bewdley, Ludlow, Bishop's Castle and Montgomery to Newtown. After that it was difficult. Hardly anyone, they were told, ventured across the wild mountains west of Newtown. Undismayed, father and daughter engaged a coach and four and drove on. They came via Llanidloes to Llangurig just as we do today. But about four miles up the Wye from Llangurig they left the present road and struck south-west over the hills along a track which is unknown to the modern traveller and which dropped them into the valley of the Ystwyth. They slept that night at a very poor inn at Ysbyty Ystwyth for the sound reason that 'if the traveller sleeps between Llanidloes and Aberystwyth it must be here', though it meant sleeping in the same room as the landlord and his family.

Having established his daughter at the Talbot Inn at Aberystwyth the father had to return home on business. Trying to find an easier way home he walked the eighteen miles to Machynlleth where, he was told, he would get a post-chaise. In this he was evidently disappointed, for we find his daughter writing later that she was 'sorry to hear that father had to walk on to Shrewsbury' (another fifty-seven miles).

Otter Encounter

The other day on one of the pools by the River Teifi where it flows through Tregaron Bog, I had the good fortune to see an otter swimming towards me. When he dived twenty yards away I thought he must have seen me; but to my surprise he surfaced only a few feet away and allowed me a pleasure one too seldom gets—that of seeing a carnivore by day at really close range. For a few seconds I experienced the strange excitement of looking into the eyes of a wild creature, eyes fuller of curiosity than fear. My impression was of a flattened, round-eyed, distinctly cat-like face, heavily whiskered. So I find it a little curious that otter in Welsh should be 'dwrgi', the water-dog.

Though the otter left the pool and disappeared into the dense aquatic vegetation, I had no difficulty in following his course, for it was marked for half a mile by successive displays of duck mallards that rose quacking in anxiety about their broods, easy victims I suppose for this swift-moving raptor. Seeing an otter there reminded me that the Teifi—and what more likely stretch than where it flowed through the great bog of Tregaron?—is the traditional last haunt in Britain of another master of underwater swimming, the beaver. It is remarkable that the centuries which have wiped out the beaver almost throughout Europe have left the otter still locally common.

Our Garden's Rich Harvest

This seems a suitable date to assess our little garden's autumn harvest. The failures first. Our hundred-thousand or so bees have less to show at the season's end than they had at the beginning. We feel like buying them a few jars of our neighbour's honey. On the grafted apple-tree nothing, as usual. On the Williams pear, nothing, also as usual. Damsons a few. Potatoes blighted. So far so bad, but I beg you look at the credit side.

Our rowan tree though rotten to the heart is a glory of scarlet berries and fuller of chiff-chaffs every day. Our sedums are coloured all over with red admirals, peacocks, tortoiseshells, silver-washed fritillaries and painted ladies. Yesterday there was a brimstone. Then there is our newly planted balsam poplar, perhaps not a tree you would expect to give much of a yield. Yet what was our delight last week to find lovely, pale, plump caterpillars of the poplar hawk-moth hanging from its leaves like unripe fruits. Now that they have gone to earth the tree is starting a valuable aftermath, this time of some caterpillars new to us. They are tiny, humpy and black, and disguise themselves by day as bits of dead and twisted leaf-tissue by sticking out rigidly from the withered tips of leaves. These may well prove the season's choicest crop and certainly at the moment are all the more precious because unknown.

To Harlech for the Tonic of Wildness, 1958

The recent designation of Morfa Harlech as a nature reserve is very welcome news. From now on this wild stretch of unspoilt sand-dunes, saltings and fresh marshes and all their varied animals and plants will be reasonably safe from destruction or exploitation. One has only to see the huddles of caravans that have been allowed to disfigure the coast a few miles to the south to realise what a fate hangs over all such beautiful shores.

Perhaps there is nothing very rare to be protected at Morfa Harlech. But that is not the point of most nature reserves. What matters at Harlech is that a natural place is being conserved complete with its fauna and flora.

Officially nature reserves are intended to safeguard our remnant of wild life and provide places where biologists and naturalists can pursue their studies under natural conditions. But unofficially they can provide something besides intellectual profit, something probably far more vital if less tangible. I mean what Thoreau called 'the tonic of wildness', that especial refreshment of the spirit which comes to us from getting out into the open air in a stretch of coast or country where there is not a habitation, not so much as an ice-cream stall, in sight. Perhaps we, as much as plants and animals, are in acute need of nature reserves.

Great Tides that come by Night

Though its times and heights are set down neatly in a little book they sell you for sixpence, the tide is, in fact, mysteriously unpredictable. We expect fluctuations in rough weather yet even in a dead calm an expected 27-foot tide sometimes swells up and becomes a 30-footer, presumably because of some disturbance far away. Sometimes on moonlit nights I walk across the field behind the house to the estuary to see the night tide come in. It is exciting at any time to see a great spring tide flooding the estuary and spreading a lake for miles across the saltings. But when it happens at night, under conditions of absolute calm, this silent but swift inflowing of the water is much more dramatic.

Man is not the only creature to feel a primitive excitement at the inpouring of the waters. The wading birds feel it too as they are forced back off the mud-flats, and they show it in their voices. Curlews particularly have special conversation notes with which they greet the incoming tide and it is wonderful to hear a really great flock of excited curlews being pushed steadily towards you across the moonlit saltings until they are packed together only a few yards from your hiding place. Otters too know the excitement of the spring tides and occasionally I hear one whistling or see one make a black line across the silvery water as he swims by.

Helen's Ancient Way

One of the longest Roman roads in Wales is called Sarn Helen, which means Helen's Causeway. And if you want to know who Helen (better spelt Elen) was, any Welshman will tell you. She was the Welsh wife of a Roman emperor called Macsen (i.e. Maximus) and it was she who had this great road constructed. It is a pity that this story is no more than an interesting invention. It appears in that superb collection of medieval Welsh tales, the *Mabinogion*. And although the *Mabinogion* no doubt contains folk-memories that go back to the pre-Norman world, Elen is post-Roman, invented perhaps in the days when the Roman legions were beginning to get hazy in the Welsh memory, say about 600 A.D.

But if the date of the invention of Elen is in doubt, the reason for it is clear enough. It was one of the recognised tricks of the medieval story-teller to make up tales to explain the origin of strange place-names. Obviously the name of this great road, which sounded like Sarn Elen, had to be accounted for. So this lady Elen was thought up, and all the details of how she became an emperor's wife. For what people had forgotten by, say, 600 A.D. was that the road's real name had been more like Sarn y Leon, which meant the Causeway of the Legions, just as the town of Caerleon (Castra legionum) was the Camp of the Legions.

Do Cormorants Dry Their Wings?

A sea bird that catches everybody's eye is the cormorant when it stands motionless with wings outstretched. I remember years ago on a bird identification course our instructor, an acknowledged expert, was asked why cormorants held their wings in this strange position. He gave the stock answer that cormorants dry their wings in this way, and this was accepted until later when we saw another cormorant holding its wings out during a heavy shower. Questioned about this, the instructor unblushingly claimed that this cormorant was washing its wings! Ever since then I have not only had a deep distrust of experts but have also wondered what is the real reason why cormorants hang out their wings. It happens that lately I have had the chance of watching cormorants closely from a hide, and found that their behaviour on emerging from water onto land was not at all consistent. Some opened their wings, others did not. But though I cannot explain this difference I can say that whenever a cormorant had swallowed a big fish he then went straight to a rock and immediately stretched out his wings. So it looks as if there may be a link between wing-stretching and digestion, just as if holding the wings out somehow eases pressure on the stomach. After all, vultures do this after gorging on a carcass on the plains of Africa. And in the middle of the dry season it can scarcely be suggested that vultures need to dry their wings.

Hawk-moths a'plenty

I don't ever remember a year like this for caterpillars of the eyed hawk-moth; they have been so numerous and so long-lasting. Whole branches of the sallows along the railway have been stripped of their leaves and this is the easiest clue to the presence of these great eaters. Not that they try to conceal themselves anyway. With reckless disregard of puncturing flies, birds or any other enemies, they feed in full sunlight at the ends of quite exposed twigs. It is as if they had never read the textbooks which say that these larvae hide by day lying along the central vein of the underside of a leaf, their head towards the stalk so that their transverse pale lines seem to continue the side-veins of the leaf and so achieve a marvellous camouflage. I began finding these caterpillars back in June but those early ones have long since pupated. Now it is September and still I see these splendidly huge, brilliantly green creatures that are so conspicuous against their dark-green leaves. I remember years ago a far greater burgeoning of caterpillars: that time it was of the poplar hawk-moth, scores of them in the sand-dunes, feeding on creeping willow. But the following year their numbers were quite below normal. Thus mysteriously does nature nearly always redress the balance. So I expect that next year it may be quite hard to find an eyed hawk-moth anywhere.

Mountain-top Dotterels

The other day I set off up Pumlumon to visit the source of the Severn, not having been there for many years. But I also carried with me the admittedly faint hope of seeing a bird I have always looked for in vain—a dotterel. In Wales this rare little plover has a most curious pattern of migration. Apparently on its way to and from its Arctic breeding grounds it flies from one mountain top to the next and scorns the lowlands almost completely. And Pumlumon is one of the mountains it has occasionally visited. To reach the source of the Severn used to be quite an achievement. I remember in my youth struggling with a bicycle along a rough moorland track up to the highest house, Blaen Hafren, then doing quite a climb on foot up to the source. But what changes since! Only Snowdon with its railway is easier than Pumlumon today. For now it is conifered up to the eye-brows and a forestry road goes nearly to the top. So I reached the source of the Severn in no time at all and was soon on the highest ridge searching for the elusive dotterel. But there were none. Never mind, I thought, the views are quite wonderful, especially of Aran Fawddwy standing high in the north. Returning that evening I met a friend near my home. 'Ah!' he said, 'What do you think I've seen today—eight dotterel on the summit of Aran!'

September Mistletoe

I know that it is only at Christmas that we normally ever think about mistletoe, but seeing a great round ball of it in a roadside tree this week reminded me of how rare it is in nearly the whole of Wales. The spot where I noticed it was near Abergavenny and, as you go east through that district, you see more and more of it because you are approaching Britain's best mistletoe region: the counties of Hereford, Worcester and Gloucester. There it is most abundant in old apple orchards, poplar plantations and other man-made habitats. The wilder the woodland the less the mistletoe. So in our natural forests it was probably never common and must have flourished mainly on crab apple trees. A tree on which it was probably always very rare is the oak. Back in Druidical times mistletoe was worshipped as a powerful fertility symbol because it remained mysteriously green in winter when the twigs it grew on seemed dead. So to discover mistletoe on an oak, which was itself a much revered tree, was for the Druids an event of the utmost significance. I wonder if the craftier Druids knew the trick of slitting open the bark and planting a mistletoe seed in it? Even if they did, their problems were by no means over. This works well enough with apple trees in Herefordshire but I would bet it is a different matter with oaks in Anglesey.

Bardsey's Migrant Birds

I spent last week with fellow enthusiasts at the bird observatory on Bardsey Island, one of the best spots on the Irish Sea coast to see the migration of birds, especially in autumn when they are moving multitudinously from north Europe towards the south and west. Nearly all are very common birds but if you wait long enough and watch hard enough you are fairly certain to see one or two rarities. So last week we saw amongst all the commoners a Richard's pipit, a red-breasted flycatcher and a short-toed lark, this last being Bardsey's first ever. But though it was good to see these exotics from the other side of Europe we were just as intrigued to meet with a party of nine jays that had perhaps come island-visiting from less than ten miles away and which, being thorough woodlanders, looked remarkably out of place feeding among the rocks of Bardsey Mountain. But what I always most enjoy on Bardsey is not these odd individual birds so much as the sights and calls of the flocks passing overhead, the chaffinches, greenfinches, linnets, goldfinches, bramblings, fieldfares, redwings and larks that follow each other in hastening groups every few minutes for two or three hours from dawn onwards. When you see them all streaming purposefully out into the empty loneliness of the sea with no visible land ahead, you get a real feeling of the power that lies inside the migratory urge.

A Good Summer for Waterfalls

This year we had a wet July and August. But what else should we have expected after two summers when the sun shone with such enthusiasm week after week that even here in the west the pastures were burnt brown? This year all we can do is remind ourselves that there is an enjoyable side to rain. Our garden, for instance, is producing beans at almost frightening speed. The trees, too, love every inch of rain that falls, and I do not remember seeing the woods in better health and so green with mosses that normally dry up in the spring. And some of the autumn fungi are already magnificent. I think especially of that edible toadstool, bright-orange and smelling of apricots, which for some reason is given a French name, chanterelle. Just now it is making brilliant patches of colour in the shade of the trees. But the best thing this summer has been the waterfalls and in the past few weeks I have been doing the rounds of the more famous ones in Snowdonia just as the tourists used to do a couple of centuries ago, obediently plodding or riding from one fall to the next as the guidebooks dictated. To photograph them has not been easy because the sun has rarely given a wink just when it was needed, and I suppose the lesson from this is that we should take tape recorders, not cameras, to waterfalls, and train ourselves in the appreciation of the many different types of water music, from the soft and melodious to the harsh and thunderous. They say everyone will be going abroad next year to find the sun. So we in Wales will be left in peace to enjoy our waterfalls, our mosses and our rain.

Wales, Land of Ferns

Wales is a land of ferns. Everywhere they welcome you on roadside walls, streamsides, peatbogs and hillsides. They love deep gorges and shadowy woodlands. They even wave to you from the branches of trees. One of them flourishes on the poisonous spoil heaps of lead-mines. Another hides in the caves of the misty Atlantic. A few prefer the highest, wettest, windiest and iciest terraces of the mountains. Some also flourish in gardens, invited there or not. Of these garden dwellers, none is more irrepressible than the lady ferns. When we came to live here years ago, we were delighted to see the first lady ferns arching out of the walls with graceful innocence. But they soon became discourteous to choicer neighbours and had to be reduced. Then there is the little oak fern which has long been spreading itself happily about the garden. But no matter how far it goes, I doubt if we could ever have bad feelings towards this loveliest of all Welsh ferns. It was a rescue operation that brought our largest fern into the garden. We were going past one of our local peatbogs one day when, to our horror, we saw a whole colony of the rare royal fern being ploughed up by a go-ahead farmer. So we picked up a couple of roots and brought them home, and here they flourish still. In all Britain there is no more magnificent fern than this, and its scarcity is due entirely to human destructiveness. Its true place is in the wild, not in gardens. So one of these days, when we find a secure spot, it is back to the wild that our two royal ferns will go.

Snowdonia's Rare Holly Ferns

This week I am writing my diary perched high on a mountainside near Snowdon and sitting by a very special plant, a charming little fern which, because of its prickly leaves, is known as the holly fern. Its narrow fronds are stiff, tough and leathery, their colour a lovely bright green that will deepen into a very dark green before the end of autumn. What is so special about holly fern here is its rarity. In Scotland's mountains it is more widespread, but here in Wales it is always an exciting find. There is an historical explanation for this scarcity. The uplands of Snowdonia are the nearest fern-rich mountains to south-east and central England, and it was largely from those districts that the greedy fern collectors of the Victorian age came in search of alpine specimens. Some were happy to gather only fronds, though that was bad enough, but many were intent on uprooting the ferns and carrying them off to their gardens and greenhouses. Or they acquired them from mountain guides. In the 1840s you could buy holly fern at sixpence a root on the summit of Snowdon. The fern mania lasted many decades. In the 1880s collectors were still being advised not to go to the mountains without hammers and chisels to get at the holly ferns and other inhabitants of the rocks. So though there is much that conservationists may not like about the present scene, at least we don't have to meet people coming down Snowdon loaded with baskets of ferns.

A Nonconformist Greenshank

As I walk along the edge of the estuary I hear the ringing calls of greenshanks far out across the mud-flats. Hereabouts this is a real sound of autumn, but you can hear it also in spring if you go to those spacious moorlands of northern Scotland that are now being so shamefully destroyed to create ever vaster plantations of hideous conifers. (How can we have the nerve to blame those who are clearing the tropical forests when we are annihilating our own last wilderness areas as fast as we can?) Although the greenshank is mainly a bird of the wildest places my most vivid greenshank memory is of a bird which years ago took up temporary residence on one of our local housing estates. For nearly a month this eccentric greenshank deserted the nearby estuary in favour of a life on the little lawns of suburbia where he fed exclusively on earthworms extracted from the turf with great expertise. He became amazingly tame, taking no notice at all of passing cars, barking dogs, nor the noise of children, radios and vacuum cleaners. Cats stalked him. So did photographers. Infants tried to catch him. Groups of people stood to watch him. He became so well known that, if you couldn't find him, there was usually someone who could tell you whose lawn he was last seen on. But he evidently felt the call of the wild at last. Or else worms were getting scarce as winter approached. One day he was seen flying away high above the houses towards the south, presumably on his way to warmer lands.

A World Fit for Cabbage Whites

It has been a year of white wings above the cabbage patch. Week after week the white butterflies laid a phenomenal number of eggs on the brassicas and whole rows of cabbages were reduced to shreds. Yet, one day, when I went to Llandudno, where the cliffs were yellow with wild cabbages, I could see very little sign of caterpillar attack. Why was this? For an answer I turned to a lady called Anne Pratt who many years ago wrote volumes about wild flowers and who, I remembered, was an admirer of wild cabbage, which she describes as not only the chief adornment of the limestone cliffs but also the origin of all our garden cabbages. But not even Anne Pratt could stomach the bitter flavour of wild cabbage which she claims is probably what gives the plant such immunity from pests. She once saw a cliffside garden where the brassicas were totally destroyed by caterpillars, while the wild cabbages flourished unscathed on the rocks all round. Evidently down the ages, as we have cultivated ever more palatable cabbages in our gardens, we have deprived them of the pungency which in the slow course of evolution they had developed as their natural protection. In so enormously increasing the number of cabbages in the world, we must have hugely multiplied the population of the caterpillars that feed on them. So maybe in the forested days of prehistory the cabbage butterflies were rare insects mainly confined to limestone sea cliffs, struggling to survive on wild cabbage and hating every mouthful of the dreadful stuff.

Sir Peter Scott: In Memoriam, 1989

A sad news item on Wednesday was the death of Sir Peter Scott, to whom David Bellamy payed fitting tribute on the radio. I remember Peter Scott coming here many years ago to advise on how best to protect the wild geese of mid-Wales. His lecture in a village hall was a masterly performance unaided by technology. With just a blackboard and a piece of chalk he created wonderful drawings of his beloved geese in a few seconds as he talked. I am sure no one went home from that lecture without learning something of the magic of wild geese. And in due course a national nature reserve was created on the estuary here, one of whose chief objects is the protection of geese. The process of education continues. Last weekend we had David Bellamy here to open a new reserve of the Dyfed Wildlife Trust and give us a magnificent talk. There is no doubt we need men like Scott and Bellamy to come and harangue us from time to time. But though the generals are important, in the end it's the troops on the ground who win the battle. As Bellamy pointed out, every part of Britain now has a local wildlife trust. No local trust, however, is going to have a great impact on events unless it has the support of truly large numbers of people. So what about you, gentle reader? Details of your local wildlife trust can be obtained from the Royal Society for Nature Conservation, The Green, Nettleham, Lincoln, LN2 2NR.

A Thankless Task

When a visitor here this week remarked that he had just seen a red squirrel in a nearby wood I felt I had to point out to him that if he really had seen a red squirrel it was the first record for a great many years. Our visitor then rather coldly assured me that he knew a red squirrel when he saw one and the conversation went quickly on to other topics. All the same, the identification of our squirrels is not as clear cut as their names suggest because both species can partly change colour with age and season. Young grey squirrels, for instance, sometimes look more red than grey. So it is clearly wise to be sceptical about reports of red squirrels in districts where they have not been seen for decades. Of course, some observers can never admit they are wrong. I am reminded of the days long ago when I used to collect the county bird records, a thankless occupation during which I offended quite a few people by rejecting their reports because they were insufficiently substantiated. I well remember displeasing a lady who for two or three springs in succession reported (without any evidence) seeing in her garden a red-breasted flycatcher, a truly rare bird in Wales. Long after this lady had ceased all correspondence with me I heard through others that even having gone to live in another county she still went on seeing her flycatchers, complete with red breasts, every April. Now she has gone to Heaven but I've no doubt she embarrasses the bird-recording angel up there with reports of celestial rarities. I pray he is more tactful with her than I ever was.

OCTOBER

Gardening for Nature

(This was my first 'Country Diary'—it appeared in the *Manchester Guardian* in October 1957)

From spring to autumn our little mountainside garden has a compelling attraction for butterflies and moths. I think there are two reasons for this. First, it provides an oasis of fragrance in a desert of brackeny slopes and sheep-nibbled pastures, the nearest garden being a mile away down the valley, while behind us the Welsh mountains climb away almost houseless, certainly gardenless, for twenty miles or more. Second, we try to grow flowers which have strong attractions for insects, flowers which we would replace by species of more distinction were it not for the butterflies. But how can we get rid of our purple aubretias when in spring they bring us clouds of pearl-bordered fritillaries? How cut back our buddleias in March and so prevent their flowering in June just when the dark-green fritillaries would be on them?

Now on quiet, sun-filled days the Michaelmas daisies, especially the scented varieties, bring us coppers, tortoiseshells, peacocks, red admirals, commas and an occasional belated brimstone. But the superb insect-enticer in the past few weeks has been *Sedum spectabile:* this not only attracts butterflies from miles around but is a handsome plant too, if a little stolid, with its fleshy leaves and flat cymes of pink flowers. Then by night there are the white tobacco flowers under our windows—the whites seem more scented than the coloured—and since one October night they lured down a convolvulus hawk-moth for us we always hope the miracle may happen again.

Red Admirals Love Goat Moths

Just outside our garden gate is an aged birch whose thick gnarled bole is bored near the ground with the holes of the goat-moth caterpillar, borings which go deep into the trunk and are wide enough to insert a finger in. At the entrances to these holes there accumulates a pulpy substance which, if you bend down and sniff at it, you find has an unpleasant smell. But though the human nose cannot detect this scent beyond a few inches range the red admiral butterflies can pick it up at great distances; when it is plentiful you can see them on sunny autumn days fluttering upwind through the trees with rather uncertain flight but all converging at last upon this one birch. Day after day there may be a dozen or two close together on the trunk drinking at the peculiar juices draining from the caterpillars' tunnels or simply resting there without sipping.

Perhaps the smell of the goat-moth holes acts for the red admirals as a sort of rotten-fruit concentrate. Certainly it lures them far better than even a rotten pear does. It is an attraction similar to that of the putrefying corpses on gamekeepers' gibbets which in certain woods of the south of England are said to attract down the purple emperor.

Road to an Ancient Land

If you enjoy following old roads with plenty of history and no motor cars along them I recommend the one which climbs north out of Bont-ddu on the Mawddach estuary, makes for a gap in the mountains and then goes several miles north-west across as rude and rough a district as exists in all Wales. Finally it descends to the coast.

Unmistakably the signs are all about you that ancient man had far more use for this wild upland shelf than any subsequent age has found. There are two great cairns, one of which is fifty yards long and must once have been much longer before it was despoiled for the building of modern field walls. Both of them contain elaborate burial chambers. There are stone circles, cromlechs and isolated monoliths; and two of the adjacent hills are crowned with hill forts and encrusted with rings of stones.

Men who were accustomed to express their deepest thoughts and feelings in terms of stone monuments could not have failed to be drawn to such country as this. For nowhere could you find more large loose rocks lying about. There are in places acres and acres of ground from which the soil, if ever there was any, has been deeply and entirely eroded to expose a chaos of slabs and boulders with spaces below them going deep into the earth, as if some enormous primeval city had been shattered by an earthquake and never rebuilt.

Indian Summers, Equinoctial Gales

Indian summers are delightful compensations for autumn's shortening days, rising winds and falling temperatures. They are strange brief interludes, the results of quite irregular intrusions of Azorean anticyclones into the North Atlantic. Their appearances are traditionally, though not in fact, associated with the feasts of certain saints. In Wales it is Michaelmas (29 September) which is said to bring hope of the first spell of fine autumn weather: Haf Bach Mihangel, the Little Summer of Saint Michael, it is called. The date is interesting, approximating as it does to the equinox, traditional period for dirty weather. Actually the records, though not quite vindicating the Welsh faith in St Michael's halcyon weather, will certainly have no truck with equinoctial gales. September is, in fact, shown to be a quieter month than most. So it is with the feasts of St Luke (19 October) and St Martin (11 November): they do sometimes coincide with periods of Indian summer.

I write these words sitting in the garden with the sun hot on my bare arms. The long soft flutings of a robin come from the hedge and there is a spring-like carolling of a woodlark overhead. Silver-Y moths and bees blunder hastily among the cone-shaped flowers of the rudbeckias. For an instant a wall butterfly suns itself on my page. But Indian summers are fleeting. Already the forecasters are talking of approaching fronts and by the time my words are in print these sunny hours may have a dreamlike remoteness.

Churchyards for Wildlife

I hope that naturalists who are looking round for places suitable for turning into nature reserves will not forget our village churchyards, for many of these have the makings of the perfect sanctuary. Admittedly some are obviously unsuitable. But there is many a solitary, rustic churchyard which, with the introduction of more trees and shrubs (especially berried kinds such as cotoneasters), would become a welcome refuge for wildlife.

There could be a lavish provision of nest-boxes for tits, robins, flycatchers, even owls. But failing boxes a mere slab of wood so fixed to a tree as to leave a gap behind it is good enough for many small birds, especially creepers and wrens, as I saw in a Breconshire churchyard last week. Of course many ancient churchyards need no conversion at all. Time itself has made sanctuaries of them. Their great yews are full of birds' nests; their hollow elms all hoot with tawny owls; their overgrown corners are a haven for small mammals, rare insects and a most interesting assortment of wild flowers. The church itself, to be ideal, should house a family of white owls, an assembly of jackdaws and a varied company of bats, swifts, swallows and martins. So our churches could go on for ever being in a real sense centres of life. So maybe there is no need to despair so much about the waning of human congregations.

Suddenly We all have Thorn-apples, 1959

A wild plant in the news just now is thorn-apple, a strange-looking alien that may turn up anywhere but is normally rather rare, for it prefers a warmer climate than it would usually find in most of Britain. But it must be a remarkable opportunist, for during this wonderful summer it has seeded itself over wide areas where it is normally unknown. I had never seen it till this year, when one has appeared outside our garden gate. It is almost a shrub in size and easily overtops the jungle of weeds among which it sprawls.

Thorn-apple is cut out for fame. It is of unusual appearance because of its extremely prickly fruits the size of golf balls. What is more, as with its cousin, deadly nightshade, unpleasant things have happened to those who ventured to eat it, be they man or beast.

I know I ought to have uprooted and burnt it, growing as it is in a field pastured by cattle, sheep and horses. But as it was two feet tall when I found it, it must have been there a couple of months already; yet not a leaf on it has been nibbled. Since then I have repeatedly seen bullocks sniff at it and move hastily away. All the same, as a precaution I have now caged it in so that I can observe its progress, for I hope its fruits will ripen and split open before the frosts.

In Praise of Field-mice

In creating a garden in the wilds we created also a field-mouse paradise. And expel mice as quickly as we may, they are all soon replaced. So we resign ourselves to peaceful coexistence and a tulip-less, crocus-less garden;

and learn to love our mice. For the long-tailed field-mouse is an admirable creature. Catch one alive and see how wonderfully full of life he is, this big, nervous mouse climbing rapidly all over the walls and roof of the cage. Pick him up and he will give you a sharp little bite, jump to earth and go bounding away in athletic, kangaroo-like leaps. A pity he is not more trusting, for he is a creature of beauty with his shapely ears, large lustrous eyes and a silky brown coat divided so neatly from white breast and belly.

He is an adventurous, enterprising mouse. To include our garden in his province is not enough: he must climb our walls and nibble every apple on our cordon tree. Then he comes indoors and plays the house-mouse to perfection, enlivening our evenings with heavy rustlings in the waste-paper basket. But to hear the field-mice really in action, go and sleep in the woods without a tent and hear them pattering on the dry leaves all about you.

What a Green World!

Wet or dry, October is a good month. It is the month when we are treated to a real wealth of colour. We enjoy spring when the world turns green; but what a pity that there has to be so much green and that it lasts so long. It is all because of this stuff they call chlorophyll. I always think the Creator overdid it a bit when he thought up chlorophyll as the bright idea of his leaf chemistry. For it meant that though all the colours of the rainbow were available, practically every growing plant had to be green. So we get green fields, green woods, green hills, green valleys for months on end until October when the monotony of it all breaks up and we are granted a short blaze of other colours. So a cheer for autumn leaves. And another for autumn toadstools. Certainly, whether we dare to eat them or not, we should be grateful for our toadstools if only because, free from the tyranny of chlorophyll, they can express themselves in whatever colours they like—bright yellows, oranges, reds and purples.

Badgers, Foxes, Cats—All at the Feast

Why go all the way to the woods to watch badgers? Why not entertain them in your garden and observe them from the comfort of your living-room? This is what some friends of mine do nearly every evening. It began one night when, in the light that was shed on their terrace through the French window, they were delighted to see a fox cleaning up scraps put out for the birds.

A few nights later there were two foxes. A few months later a whole family of foxes were coming for meat put out for them. Act II starts with the arrival of the first badger, much to the obvious disgust of the foxes. But badgers don't give a damn about foxes and soon there was often more than one badger on the scene and my friends frequently sat at their window watching a very unusual play featuring both foxes and badgers.

Then last week Act III began. Attracted by all the meat scraps, the village cats arrived. If foxes were present, the cats just prowled around in the outer darkness. For cats and foxes generally don't agree. But what about cats and badgers? At the moment when the first badger met the first cat my friends held on to their chairs in excitement, fearing to see the cat torn limb from limb. But not at all. The two animals met with the utmost civility and actually rubbed noses!

After that, what next?

In Wildlife is the Sanity of the World

My memory goes back to a time when hundreds of acres along our local estuary were a wide wilderness of rushes and sedges, the haunt of ducks, geese, waders and wetland plants. Then, aided by a vast Government handout, an enterprising consortium drained nearly all of it and turned it into marginal farming land. And now all that is left is about fifteen acres of snipe marsh. But they won't be there for long. I now hear that even this pathetic remnant cannot be spared by agriculture. Along will come more ditching machines, more pipes, more Government money. In will come the cattle and out will go the snipe. I know I must be a real simpleton but I really am bewildered by the logic of our agricultural lords and masters. Europe, we are told, is suffering under the burden of a beef mountain. And our Government says we must reduce public spending. Where then is the sense of giving tax-payers' money to farmers to produce more beef? Would it not be better to let the land lie fallow until it is really needed? And if the Government is dying to give money away then let it go to nature conservation. Let us not only keep our snipe marshes, let us create some new ones. After all, as increasing numbers of people are beginning to realise, wildlife is an important product, an integral part of the sanity of the world.

A Hungry Heron from Norway

Recently an exhausted heron with a Norwegian ring on his leg was brought in to the RSPB Reserve here. Though not seriously injured he was too weak to take food and it had to be pushed down his throat. For many days he remained extremely feeble, living a skulking life in the woodshed. But suddenly after about a fortnight he emerged. He came tottering out and actually picked up a piece of fish I had accidently dropped. After that he did not look back. No more pushing food down his gullet. All I had to do was to throw it to him. His legs grew stronger, his breast fatter and wing-flapping exercises began. A week later he flew away over the trees to the river and we bade him farewell. But evidently he did not prove much of a fisherman. Four days later he was back, flying in without hesitation and obviously expecting a hand-out. Now he seems to have settled for a life part-wild, part-tame. He still goes off fishing but in a day or two he turns up for his rations. As I write this sitting in the garden he is standing on the cottage roof looking distinctly hungry. Does he wonder where his next meal is coming from? I certainly do with fish the price it is. So the Norwegian Embassy can expect a massive bill for sardines in a few months' time.

A Question of Stone Loaches, 1970

The standard work on the animals of north Wales was written by H. E. Forrest in 1907. Since then, the status of many species must have changed. I was reminded of this last Sunday, on the banks of the Dyfi River. My companion happened to relate how, as a child thirty years ago, he used to turn over stones in the river bed and find a little fish called the loach. Full of book learning, I felt impelled to doubt this. I told him there are not supposed to be any loaches in the Dyfi. According to H. E. Forrest, I pointed out, the loach is common in east Wales, but not found further west than Bala. My friend looked contemptuous. Come on, he said, I will show you loaches. He began turning over flat stones in the river, carefully replacing them as a naturalist should. But he turned many and found only troutlets that darted away. His face began to look doubtful. More stones were turned, but still no loach. Then, just as we were giving up, he gave an exclamation of triumph. I went over, and there sure enough, was a genuine loach, a little pale fish with faint bars down the back and whiskers at the side of the mouth. So now the question arises: did loaches happen to get into the Dyfi between say 1910 and 1940? Or were they always there?

Churches for Tourists

It is a modern paradox that the more religion declines the more interest people show in churches: in their architecture, history, woodwork, stonework, memorials, brasses and all their various curiosities and antiquities. Such churches are churches on Sundays and museums most of the rest of the week, a fact that is resented by some clergy but accepted by most. As the philosophical parson of one of Pembrokeshire's most visited churches remarked to me recently: 'Even if Christianity dies out altogether the churches will still be valuable tourist attractions, so tourists had better help to look after them'. And this to some extent they do, though the trickle of coins they drop into the collecting boxes cannot go very far. The cost of maintaining the fabric of a church must be colossal, especially in those exposed upland districts where wind, rain and frost are excessive. I visited a little church in just such a place the other day, the famous old church of Partrishow in the Black Mountains of Breconshire, a building that typifies the church that is also a museum. Its interior is dominated by a splendid medieval screen and rood loft. There are wall paintings and old texts and one of the most ancient fonts in Wales. Outside, along the south wall, runs a long stone bench on which people sat in fine weather to hear services from the churchyard cross. The place is, in fact, a real feast of history, deserving every financial support.

The End of a Wasps' Nest

If you go badger-watching it is well to choose a quiet night. And the test of a quiet night is not whether you can hear the acorns falling. For they come bounding down from branch to branch with a clinkety-clonk you can hear from one end of the wood to the other. No, the real test of a quiet night is when you can hear the falling leaves settling on the ground several yards away. In that sort of delicious stillness you can hear the badgers beginning to stir below ground and you have good warning of the cautious grey face you soon see looking out of the burrow. But the snag about badgers' setts is that they can have many exits. Which is why the other night I was unlucky. My badgers chose to leave by a hole for which I was unsighted and I missed them completely. But by pure luck on my way home through the wood I came upon a badger digging so strenuously he did not hear my approach. I turned aside not wishing to disturb him. I knew what he was up to for I, too, had found the wasps' nest in the bank just there. Going back this morning I found a great cavity there, and the wasps' nest is a complete wreck with a few surviving wasps clinging to the ruins dejectedly. A sad end to a beautiful city.

Fear Not the Toadstool

Now the fungi are appearing in the woods. All along my path through the larches this morning I found quantities of pure white toadstools shaped like inside-out umbrellas and looking most inviting. But did I gather them for my lunch? Not likely. For am I not British and full of terror at the thought of eating such vegetables? But I wish I were not. I wish I had inherited the knowledge of fungi that many, perhaps most, of the world's peoples seem to possess almost by instinct. The peasants of Russia and other North European countries make a great thing of harvesting the fungi of autumn and storing them for the winter. The tribes of Africa eat their toadstools with relish. And so throughout the world as far as I know. But not the British. Why not? It can't simply be because we have become so industrialised, for the ten per cent who are still country folk have little knowledge or tradition of eating fungi. Nor is it an Anglo-Saxon peculiarity. The Celtic fringe seems just as frigid towards the fungi. The few British I know who regularly gather toadstools do it intellectually, so to speak. They have learned about them from books not from their forebears. And my guess is that they really trust very few species whereas the Continental peoples seem to eat nearly all they can find. So perhaps it will be good for us to go into Europe after all.

What Hope for our Estuaries?

If there is one natural habitat more than most that is currently under threat it is estuaries. All round our coasts it is increasingly hard to find an estuary for which somebody has not thought up a barrage scheme. Civil engineers have no difficulty in discovering that enormous benefits would be showered on mankind if our jagged coastline could be tidied up by a vast chain of barrages. But naturalists know what very special places estuaries are as habitats for a fascinating fauna and flora that would be destroyed for ever by barrage schemes. When you think that estuaries and inlets are disappearing or are threatened all round the coasts of Europe it becomes clear that the total effect on nature of this revolution is likely to be enormous. The most obvious example is the effect on the vast numbers of estuary-feeding wading birds. What will happen to them when their mud-flats have gone from the Wash, the Solway, Morecambe Bay and the Dee, not to mention the German, Dutch and French coasts? One can only hope that all future schemes will include provision for the preservation of part of the natural saline habitat. And, above all, that some estuaries will be completely left for the tides to play with as they have from the beginning. Surely we don't want future children to have to ask questions like: 'But, daddy, what was an estuary?'

Splendours of Cader Idris

As I climbed Cader Idris with a friend last Sunday I thought of Thomas Pennant, who in 1773 was one of the first to describe an ascent of this mountain. He struck a wet day and got no view. But he was able to look down into those glacial cirques that have gouged out precipices on either side of the narrow summit ridge. He saw them as 'a sort of theatre with a lake at the bottom'. He was also impressed by the chaos of naked rocks that lay in all directions; and quite astutely for those early days he suggested that these rocks might have come out of a volcano. Pennant climbed the north side of Cader but we went up from the south. For us the day was fine and there were many hill walkers enjoying the warm autumn sunshine. Not as formidable as Snowdon nor nearly as crowded, and unpolluted by a railway and summit café, Cader gets deservedly more popular year by year. My companion on

Sunday was a Canadian lady with experience of far higher mountains than those of Britain. Yet she found Cader Idris full of appeal because its rugged treelessness gives it true mountain qualities. In North America there are many ranges that are disappointing to climb because they are forested to the summit and give you no view at all. But from Cader on a clear day you see across all Snowdonia and central Wales to similar bare heights, all of which are marvellous viewpoints. You would need a long lifetime to visit every one of them.

NOVEMBER

Using One's own two Feet

The night before last a polecat rippling across the road in front of my car was so clearly picked out by the headlamps that I could see not only his long, dark, low-slung shape but even the creamy under-fur that is a peculiarity of this superficially black animal. Polecats are far commoner round here than most people suspect, but they were better known last century when both they and pine martens were regular objects of the chase. An enormous amount of hunting on foot used to take place on the Welsh uplands and though we may regret that so much energy was not expended more worthily we have to admit that the people of those days did learn through hunting to make real use of their legs and their lungs.

Here, for instance, is an entry from a Welsh hunting diary: 'By measurement on the Ordnance map I had walked at least 50 miles over the roughest country . . . I never felt such heat'. (It was in August.) Perhaps to keep going all day in the excitement of the chase is understandable. It was the walks home at the end of the day that would defeat us today. 'Walked back to Aberystwyth, 19 miles' or 'Walked home via Talyllyn and Machynlleth by road about 37 miles'. Who today could do it? But the note I most prize in this diary runs: 'A small boy named Barge followed the hounds all day with bare feet.'

A Nonchalant Polecat

Carnivorous animals frequently pass by or through our garden. Nearly all come by night and are rarely even glimpsed. We know otters by their shrill whistlings in the outer darkness. Foxes sloping by at dawn leave a smell that may hang about the rest of the morning. Our badgers, though there are plenty on the hill, are usually unseen beings which when surprised go crashing away through the bracken like bears. Occasionally a sharp little face has inspected us by day from a hole in the wall and silently retired—and that was a weasel.

But this week we had our first daylight visit from an animal we had thought strictly nocturnal, the polecat. We watched him hunting nonchalantly through the garden, evidently in search of rat or mouse. His fur was beautiful, shining and very dark but showing at some angles a hint of white depths under the black outer hairs. His ears were conspicuously edged with white against the blackness of his head and there was a jaunty white tip to his nose. At one point he had to pass within a yard of me to get round the end of a wall, which he did without sign of fear. In fact, he paused a few seconds and literally looked me up and down in a matter-of-fact sort of way before he went on and disappeared into the woodshed with the air of one who knew his way about perfectly.

A Poet's Grave?

This week, on a rare sunny morning, I followed our alleged Roman road till I reached its highest point. Here at the wayside is a tumulus of unknown antiquity, long despoiled of its contents. Through excavation its centre is now a hollow instead of a hillock, and in that hollow lie the four slabs of an open grave. This narrow slit in the earth, they say, was the last resting place of that shadowy, sixth-century bard, Taliesin, though it seems more likely that the occupant of this tomb predeceased Taliesin by one or two thousand years.

It was a perfect morning. In the sun-drenched upland silence the songs and liquid calls of several woodlarks came clear on the air. There were whispered notes of migrating chaffinches overhead and the faint nasal shrieks of bramblings. The hills rising to the east had their sides burnished with sunlit bracken and cairn beyond cairn stood outlined along their tops. Below me to the west lay the wide estuary of the Dyfi, where a silvery tide was slowly flooding the last sandbanks. In the perfection of the present moment it hardly seemed to matter who had occupied the tumulus. Whoever he was, stone age or dark age, sinner or saint, his troubles were over long since. But if he was not a poet he ought to have been, for no place could be more worthy of a poet's grave.

Irrepressible Americans, 1957

With the sighting this autumn of a party of five grey squirrels and numerous records of others seen or killed here and around Dolgellau, the final establishment of the species in this part of Wales may be said to have begun and the period of infiltration to have ended. This infiltration has been instructive. It is now some years since individual grey squirrels, shadowy and elusive pioneers, began to be reported here. But their advance has never appeared steady. Several times they have seemed to die out but always they have eventually been replaced.

So three-quarters of a century after its introduction into England the American species conquers Wales to the coast. Compared with its rapid advance across the Midlands and into the border counties its progress since then has been slow. This was natural enough, impeded as it was by a barrier of difficult, treeless country. But it was here that the grey squirrels showed their adaptability by trekking out of the woodlands up into mountain country and so down into west Wales. One of them was trapped when crossing a high Montgomeryshire moorland some years ago. However much one may regret the advance of this squirrel it is difficult not to marvel at its success.

The Grey Squirrel settles in, 1959

It is just two years since I recorded in this diary that grey squirrels had really begun to entrench themselves in this westermost strip of mid-Wales. Now, besides becoming ever more plentiful, they are getting less timid, a sure sign that they are settling down and beginning to feel confident in their hold on the place. I have read that there are parts of the world where even herring gulls are retiring, wary and rather silent because they are there on the fringe of their range and therefore scarce; a dominated instead of a domineering species.

And so until recently were our grey squirrels. We knew they were here but they kept extremely aloof. But now, quite suddenly, they are beginning to show the other side of their nature: that boldness and familiarity which if encouraged would make them more like the favourite pets they used to be in the London parks.

So early one morning recently a grey squirrel scuttled along our bedroom window-sill; a few days later one raced across the garden; another coolly showered me with half-chewed pine-cones as I stood and looked up at him. And I doubt if it is the slightest use killing them. Tens of thousands have been killed, but that has not stopped their advance, probably not even slowed it. Think of the millions of rabbits that used to be trapped. Did that affect their numbers at all?

'The Dissemination of New Beauties'

Do you, as you go through the countryside, scatter the seeds of lovely foreign plants in the hope that they will grow to beautify the wayside in future years? If so, and if you are found out, you will certainly earn the loathing of botanists for tampering with the natural order of things, or what's left of it. But probably you are innocent of such crimes against nature. Even so, your grandfather may not have been: for it seems there was quite a fashion at one time for 'The dissemination of new beauties over our native-land' as one of its champions put it. Not that much real damage seems to have been done, but all the same the practice not surprisingly had some curious consequences.

There was, for instance, the botanist who recorded in a nature journal last century that he had found that alien, the ivy-leaved toadflax, growing apparently native on rocks near Barmouth. Imagine his pleasure at discovering what was then a rare plant in Wales until he read in the next number of the journal the following letter from a correspondent: 'I here declare that several years ago in one of my numerous tours, I carried a box of seeds of this beautiful plant, which I distributed in appropriate places on rocks, ruins, churches, castles and bridges where I have since beheld it thriving to my fullest satisfaction. I particularly remember sowing it on the rocks he mentions'.

Dormice Indoors

I suppose many naturalists who live outside the Amersham-Wendover-Whipsnade triangle envy those within it their population of edible dormice, naturalised in that one small area and nowhere else in Britain. But what a misfortune that it has the habit of taking up winter quarters in people's roofs, where its bumpings and scufflings bring it unpopularity and persecution.

I always thought that this habit of entering houses in autumn distinguished the edible from our native dormouse; but having just received a common dormouse from a lady who found it commencing hibernation in her bedroom last week I see I have been misinformed. She first discovered it when it leapt out of a sock that was being taken out of a cupboard. Then she lost it somewhere behind the furniture, only to rediscover it that night under her mattress. As this is not the first time she has found dormice in her bedroom, the house-entering habit is perhaps quite well developed. The house is adjacent to an oakwood (whence no doubt the dormice), and the espalier fruit-trees that cover the walls to the eaves were a perfect ladder for this nimble, yellow-brown, lustrous-eyed little athlete. He sits on my table as I write this note, tame already and calmly eating a raisin. No wonder dormice were once popular pets.

A Gathering of Seals, 1960

Nature, it has been suggested, has been less interfered with along the sea cliffs than in any other habitat, and I could well believe this as I walked along a part of the Welsh coast one warm, sunny day last weekend. A whole flock of ravens croaked overhead; I saw peregrines, kestrels and sparrowhawks; choughs played in the sea-wind, their bright-red legs catching the sun as they circled round; a big, greyish fox leapt out of the dead bracken and raced away along the cliff path; and though I did not see any badgers there were signs of them everywhere, for badgers are great cliff-top haunters.

But it was when I looked down over the cliff edge that I got the day's big surprise. On a wide, flat rock exposed by the falling tide was a splendid assembly of grey seals that had come out of the water to sun themselves. In fact, there were so many that when I tried to photograph them I had to retire a hundred yards up the cliff slope in order to get them all into the field of my telephoto lens. I counted sixty on that rock alone, another twenty on adjacent rocks, and these with others scattered about in the water must have totalled nearly a hundred. This was either a very unusual gathering or, what is more likely, there has been a most welcome increase in our seals during the last few years.

Our Last Shire-horse, 1960

Till lately a splendid black draught-horse lived in retirement in the fields about our house. He was stolid, monolithic, aloof, living much within his private, equine ruminations: an accepted feature of the landscape, like the rocks and trees among which he lived, and almost as unmoving. In winter he held himself stern to wind and took the weather as it came across the estuary marshes. In summer's heat he stood day after day upon a little hill for there he caught the fullest delight from whatever breeze was passing. Then a few weeks ago he took sick of a chronic foot complaint and it was deemed best to destroy him. So perished what could well be the last great shire-horse ever to set foot in these fields, for hereabouts at least, these great, feathery-legged, earth-shakers will soon seem as outlandish as dinosaurs.

We tend to forget, I think, not only how recently but how quickly the big farm horse was dispensed with. Though some tractors were in service during the First World War yet even till the mid-thirties you could still evaluate a farm by the number of its horses. An eight-horse farm you held in fair respect. A sixteen-horse farm you spoke of almost with reverence. Yet only ten years later, the Second World War having virtually completed the mechanisation of our farms, you could scan a whole countryside in vain for a glimpse of a horse at work.

What use old Diaries?

Naturalists are sometimes great diarists. Or if not great they are persistent. For maybe sixty years a chap will write down a daily miscellany of what seem rather pointless observations about plants, birds, mammals, insects, fish or merely the weather, pointless because he hardly ever refers to them again. Never mind, diary-keeping amuses him and does no harm. And it's always possible that when he dies his journals will get preserved in a library somewhere. There they may lie neglected for half a century but eventually somebody feels inquisitive enought to dip into them. The dross of fifty years ago, like old bottles, has acquired an unexpected value. These thoughts occur to be because I am just now reading the life-long diaries of a local naturalist who flourished earlier this century. J. H. Salter, Professor of Botany at Aberystwyth, was a true all-rounder. Wandering the lanes and woods he identified birds, reptiles, mammals, moths and beetles just as easily as plants. For many of these species there has been little change since his day. But some have gone. The corn buntings, woodlarks, shrikes and some of the plants he mentions are not of our time. The world of nature he knew already seems a little unreal and will be even more interesting to readers fifty years from now. So, gathering his little daily store of notes, our diarist, without realising it, was writing a quite unique kind of history.

Encounter with an Owl

I stand in a tree-sheltered spot where the wood meets the marsh, my gumboots in water from the melting snow. In the square mile of rushes and flood pools between the wood and the estuary nothing moves, nothing lives. It is dismal, cold and wet and there is nothing. But I wait. For this is the barn owl's hunting ground where he makes a careful patrol several times a day during winter, though in summer he is so nocturnal. So I wait, expecting every minute to see his white shape come floating lightly over the watery fields. But though I wait long he does not come and I wonder why. Then I happen to turn round and I find the reason: he is there already, not thirty yards away just inside the wood, staring at me from a branch, a pure white owl on the red branch of a pine. Through my binoculars I look into those large, round eyes. They have the disturbing quality of all predators' eyes but being dark seem fairly mild compared with the black-centred, yellow, penetrating eyes of short-eared owls which really are rather alarming to see at close range. Then as if feeling himself at a disadvantage being stared at by binoculars the owl turns round and flies away. But no, that describes how a crow or a pigeon would depart. I should say rather that one moment the owl is on the branch. Then he is not.

Walk to a Moorland Ruin

Wherever I went the normally dry and springy hillside turf squirted water from under my boots. But what else to expect after a month that left us with twenty inches of rain? Never mind, the sun shone now. Sunshine. Something we had almost forgotten about. But now here it was, a cloudless blue sky and the sparkle and glint of sunshine on tree and rock and grass. I had walked several miles up the valley, up through oak dingles loud with waterfalls and then up hawthorn-scattered slopes. I had passed the last inhabited house (there are only two in all the valley) and now, alone with the sheep, the gorse and the heather I had reached the highest house of all, a house where not even the oldest man in the parish remembers anybody living, a roofless house empty perhaps a hundred years but its walls still intact, a house with russet hills all round except where it looked down its valley to a perfect view of the far-off Dyfi estuary. The most tattered peacock butterfly imaginable—a miracle how it could fly—settled by me on the doorstep. So near the end of its life yet clearly enjoying every second of that splendid sunshine. And so time passed. Only a near-dead butterfly, a house in ruins, the gurgle of a stream in the bracken, a raven croaking and somersaulting overhead, the sun warm on my arm.

Away from it all?

Today, a gang has been cutting trees in a nearby plantation. Sadly, I recall the time when timber felling was a fairly quiet occupation. All we used to hear was the steady thump of an axe followed by a swish and smack as the tree came down. After that, a few more gentle axe noises as branches were lopped, then the calls of men urging horses to drag away the pole. But today's operations began with the hideous snarl of a power-saw, surely the worst sound, except for jet planes, ever to be inflicted on the rural scene. Then came the din of the tractor hauling the poles to the wood edge. More power sawings then cut the poles into logs. Next the logs were fed into a thunderous machine that shredded the bark off them. After that more tractor work got the logs to the road. I report these things because I know that even these days there are many townsfolk who cling to the myth that the countryside is a haven of peace where on retirement they are going to find their dream cottage. Before they venture forth from their perhaps fairly quiet suburb, I suggest they make sure that their proposed rural retreat is free from the following: power saws, tractors, military aircraft, helicopters, milk lorries, cattle trucks, oil tankers, motor bikes, speed boats, car rallies, shot guns, crow scarers, clay-pigeon shoots and motorised go-karts. Or, less difficult, they should get some ear plugs.

Seen any Gold Torcs lately?

Few prehistoric objects are more valuable than those hoops of twisted gold called torcs, which were evidently turned out in some numbers during the Bronze Age. Their use has been disputed: but, whether they were personal adornments or had perhaps some religious significance, it is certain that they were handed on from the Bronze to the Iron Age and that Celts, Romans, Saxons, Danes and Normans have all loved them dearly ever since. No doubt these torcs have often been coveted, stolen and hidden—sometimes by people who never returned to recover their loot. So down the centuries torcs have come to light in many places. Farmers have ploughed them out of fields, shepherds have discovered them among the mountain rocks; they have been found hidden in cellars, gardens and crannies under stones. One sold lately had been used as a loop to fasten a farm gate in Flintshire and it took the sharp eye of a gipsy to detect that it was gold not iron. Doubtless others have been quietly disposed of by melting without archaeologists ever hearing of them. This is what evidently happened to the wonderful gold hoard discovered by workmen in Denbighshire in 1782. Few details are known about it, but it included no fewer than four torcs, seven armlets and a massive chain. So maybe you should go and look at that bit of wire you looped over the gate last week!

A Great Acorn Harvest (1980)

This is one of those fruitful autumns when you crunch acorns under your feet wherever you go through the oak-wood. Millions of acorns almost none of which will ever grow up to be an oak because today's world has less and less room for oaks and other large, broad-leaved trees. Yet though the great acorn harvest produces no trees, none of it is wasted or ever has been. In the Middle Ages many an oak-wood was valued less for its timber than for the number of pigs its acorns would support. And when pushed by hunger, man also kept going on an acorn diet, though it may not have entirely agreed with him. Today the acorns are left for the eager hordes of jays, rooks, wood pigeons and squirrels which take them through all the hours of daylight. Then at dusk an even greater army of acorn devourers takes over: all the wood mice, the dormice, the bank voles and even carnivores such as badgers. Wild duck also come flying into the woods for this midnight feast; I have heard of sixty acorns being found in the crop of just one duck. The production of acorns is a very irregular performance. You might suppose that a heavy crop one autumn must be followed by a poor one a year later. Usually it is, but now and then the forest springs the surprise of producing two bumper harvests in succession. This week I had a surprise of a different sort: I was shown the rare sight of quite a large stretch of land which has just been taken out of cereal production and entirely planted with oaks. What's more, it has been planted solely for the encouragement of wildlife. Not for years have I seen anything happening in the countryside quite so heartening as this.

Rowan Berries for the Birds

Once, years ago, I lived for a month in one of the remotest houses in Wales, an abandoned shepherd's house far up into the loneliness of the moorlands. The month was August and one of my most vivid memories is of a tree that grew close to the house. It was a mountain ash which no doubt had been planted there as a sort of insurance policy, for there is believed to be nothing on earth more powerful against evil spirits than a mountain ash. The tree was brilliant with red berries and from my bedroom window in the early morning I had a marvellous view of these berries being gobbled by a party of that shy mountain bird, the ring ouzel. The mountain ash has been my favourite tree ever since. On all my upland walks it has been the last tree on the way to the summit of whatever mountain I was climbing, though perhaps if was only a poor stunted half-dead thing clinging desperately to the face of a cliff. The mountain ash, if we use the name in the widest sense and so include many different species, grows wild all round the temperate world. All these species are extremely elegant, most of them offering berries for the autumn birds. As I look out of my window at this moment I see in the garden a mountain ash from the Himalayas. It has a fine crop of white berries which, one of the text books says, will last well into the winter. But they won't do that here. Quite early every autumn these white berries vanish with wondrous speed down the throats of blackbirds and thrushes.

An Evergreen Centenarian, 1989

I am delighted to hear this week that an old friend has just celebrated her hundredth birthday. Irene Vaughan now lives in Suffolk but she spent many years in west Wales where she is still well known for her knowledge of natural history in general and of wildflowers in particular, her speciality being those many wild roses which adorn our hedgerows in June and which are so difficult to name with certainty. Irene Vaughan has always been and still is a devout conservationist and in the 1940s she and her husband, the late Captain H.R.H. Vaughan, took up the cause of protecting that beautiful rare bird, the red kite, which they occasionally saw circling gracefully over their Carmarthenshire home. So was founded the Kite Committee whose efforts over the years have saved the kite from what looked like certain extinction. Besides kite protection Irene Vaughan has battled on many other conservation fronts. But she is only one of a multitude of devoted people who have done the same. 1989 has been the year when the Green movement has achieved such sudden popular recognition in Britain that the public could be forgiven for supposing that all this greenness is something new. The truth is that this abrupt outburst of verdure among politicians has come about only because for the past hundred years so many individuals have been trying to alert the world to the need for conservation in many different fields. Last century people were distressed by the slaughter of wild birds to decorate ladies' hats. Today we agonise about the rain forests. These concerns are two ends of a chain that is complete in all its links.

DECEMBER

Shelducks bring the spring

Of the ducks that will appear on people's tables at Christmas I imagine few, if any, will be shelducks. For of all our wild ducks the shelducks are the cleverest. Though large, beautiful and tempting they have managed to offset their attractiveness by a particularly neat bit of natural selection by which they have evolved a flesh that is not to man's taste. And then, just in case there may be people about so hard-pressed for a Christmas dinner that even a shelduck would do, most shelducks have arranged to be absent from their native haunts at this time of year, returning just after Christmas.

Still, there are usually a few advance individuals back by mid-December. I saw some yesterday, gleaming black and white in the sun against a dark cloud as they flew across the estuary. And though it is still December their return is always for me a signal of spring, for have they not come back to make ready for the breeding season? It will not be many weeks now before we shall be hearing their deep quackings and musical whistles as they fly low over the house in the early morning to perch in solemn little groups outside the wood, brilliant, unlikely-looking fowl—black, white, chestnut and red—to see against the greenness of fields. Then they will rise into the air and go fluttering softly down among the trees to look for nesting holes. And then it really will be spring.

Birds along the Prom

Many countries now have their national bird but when at Aberystwyth last week it occurred to me that some towns could do likewise and have their civic bird. I was leaning over the promenade rail looking at a small wader perched below me on a ledge half-way between me and the water. Yes, undoubtedly Aberystwyth's bird would be the purple sandpiper. Consistently every autumn a small party of these waders arrives at Aberystwyth from some far-off northern breeding place. There is no need to ring them to know that they are the same birds that come back year by year (with, of course, some gradual population turnover) for they make for the same patch of rocks by the pier where they feed at low tide; and when the rising water forces them off the rocks they fly to rest on exactly the same few yards of the promenade wall. The persistency with which they do this autumn after autumn is most impressive. Whether they all summer together in the Arctic we cannot know. Possibly not, because they do not all depart or arrive together. What is certain is that somehow when they leave the north they know just where they are making for. It is just as if, when they happen to meet somewhere in Greenland or Spitzbergen, they say: 'In case we miss each other on the way down, we'd all better meet by the pier at Aberystwyth about the middle of November'.

Wintering in the Valleys

Hendre and *hafod.* These are two words which once dominated the lives of upland Welsh farmers. The *hendre* was where they lived from autumn to spring, it was their main house, their lowland base, literally 'the old homestead'. But come the warmer weather, they began to itch for the grassy hills and soon the day would arrive when, all sheep, cattle, chattels and household goods assembled, they trekked for the high ground. Miles away in the uplands they had their summer dwelling, their *hafod,* a less pretentious house than the *hendre* but often beautifully sited in a sheltered *cwm* by a stream. For shade they planted a few sycamores,for these were trees that would stand in the mountain wind. So they passed the summer in traditional shepherd style keeping watch over their flocks and herds as pastoral peoples still do today in less mechanised parts of the world.

Autumn approached and it was time to leave the mountains. The *hafod* was shut up tight, the animals rounded up and back everyone came to see the winter through at the old place. I know it is practically a crime to be nostalgic about days long gone; life then, except for a favoured few, was unspeakably harsh, cruel and sordid. All the same I cannot help thinking that to winter down in the valleys and spend each summer on the hills is a sensible, natural way of living, no matter what the century.

Put your Trust in Rowan

At our gate stands a bent old rowan tree. Or call it mountain ash, witch-wood, quicken, cock-drunks, *criafolen, cerddinen* or any other of its many names. Our tree is bent not by age nor gale but because it was deliberately bent when planted years ago to form an arch with another rowan, long disappeared, that stood on the other side of the gate.

These twin trees were set there from old Celtic custom to ward off evil spirits, for the rowan from pre-Christian days has been reckoned a sovereign charm against enchantments, especially those directed at farm animals. The girl that used to fetch the cattle home carried a stick of rowan and was careful to hang it over the cowshed door during milking and use it to drive the beasts back to pasture afterwards. What's more she always carried it in her left hand.

Common as it is elsewhere in Britain, John Evelyn regarded rowan as a specially Welsh tree and refers to it as *Fraxinus Cambro-Britannica.* He evidently quaffed the now forgotten rowan beer, for he says it is 'an incomparable drink, familiar in Wales, where this tree is reputed so sacred that there is not a churchyard without one of them planted in it (as among us the Yew); so, on a certain day in the year, everybody religiously wears a cross made of the wood'. I wonder what day that was?

Restless Red-backed Rodents

I wrote here a few weeks ago of the long-tailed field-mice which, willy-nilly, we entertain in our garden in generous numbers. But we have another ounce-sized rodent which seems even more abundant: the bank-vole. It is interesting to contrast the two, for although they live close to each other, even sharing the same underground runs, they are so very different.

For instance, as we garden we never see a field-mouse for they are creatures of the night, and only after dark do we spot these white-bellied acrobats scampering away in the torchlight. But we often catch glimpses of bank-voles. They dart out of their holes, seize some morsel as if they knew exactly where to find it, then dart back: all in two seconds. But what we see is less an animal than a lightning movement of bright chestnut-red, for this is one of our few richly coloured rodents. Compared with a field-mouse a bank-vole has smaller eyes and ears, a blunter profile and is altogether more subdued, much more the 'cow-rin' tim'rous beastie', yet very confiding. Take a bank-vole out of a live-trap and he is likely to sit on your hand to wash himself, nibble at your cuff or forage nonchalantly up your arm. And when he jumps to earth he will probably amble off with none of the frantic, leaping haste of a field-mouse.

Delectable Devil's Bridge

A traveller in 1793 records how he went to see what he called 'the greatest curiosity in all Wales'. He meant the waterfalls at Devil's Bridge. For that curse of the modern countryside, the craze to visit beauty spots, was then beginning. The popularisation of beauty spots would make an interesting study. There exist enough descriptions of Devil's Bridge falls alone to fill a sizeable anthology and if placed in order of time they would tell us a lot about the evolution both of scenic taste and of descriptive English. I suspect they would also betray an impressive amount of unacknowledged literary borrowings.

Fortunately, some of these gentlemen-travellers of the past saw other things besides crags and waterfalls. A very few even noticed the local inhabitants. So our traveller of 1793 describes a dwelling at Devil's Bridge: 'A mean, little hut built entirely of dirt and weeds. It consists of two apartments, in one of which I found a horse and a cow and in the other a whole family of pigs, ducks, dogs, cats, men, women and children. The hole by which we entered served both as window and door, and a small hole at the top suffered the smoke to pass out'.

So much for the good old days. But at least you escaped one abomination then: you did not have to pay up and click through a turnstile before you could see the falls.

Those Holiday Brochures, 1961

Surely one of the most curious of trades is that of the writer of the holiday brochures which at this season are unloaded on to the public. I wonder who writes them, who has the nerve to be so outrageously over-praiseful of these places which people are annually cajoled into visiting?

Am I wrong to picture some poor cliché-haunted hack slaving away with Roget's *Thesaurus of English Words and Phrases* on his knee, grinding out truthless eulogies of places he's never seen? Unashamedly he hands out the same old super-hackneyed superlatives to convince us that it is at Barmouth or Llandudno that we shall find that perfection of beauty, climate and relaxation that, though we may not have hitherto realised it, we all need so desperately.

The weather at these places he can always recommend with particular confidence. For example, in a current publication we are informed that Aberystwyth has 'scarcely a rainy day from May to October'! Now if we did not know from unhappy experience what nonsense this is, a glance at the weather statistics would show us that the average rainfall reaches high peaks in both July and August on this coast. But I expect I am wrong about our author. Far from being a poor hack he is probably a very smart and prosperous hack who holidays in the rarely failing sunshine of Majorca while the rarely failing rains of summer beat upon the British coasts.

A Badger Falls Sick

Last weekend I nearly tripped over a badger, of all things, curled up asleep in a field. This was surprising enough, but what happened next had a touch of unreality about it. The badger ran away across the meadow but then circled right round back to me and lay down again at my feet. What an omen might have been made of that in a more credulous age by some crafty soothsayer! In fact, there used to be a dark art called gyromancy which meant prophecy by a man walking round in circles. So I daresay a badger doing the circling would have been considered even more oracular.

But as one who never touches wood and habitually walks under ladders with uncrossed fingers, I had to explain this badger's strange behaviour in terms far removed from sorcery; and I found on examination that he was a very sick animal. Every few minutes he snuffled and shook convulsively. When I tried to handle him he snapped and went racing away again but came circling back as before as if his brain were damaged. So, knowing that the first farm-hand who found him would knock him on the head (but not from mercy), I wrapped the badger in an old coat and brought him home. And here he has lain ever since on a bed of straw, silently resting and fasting; slowly recovering or slowly dying; I wish I knew.

A Badger Recovers

I can now bring a happy conclusion to the story of the badger which, as I reported in this diary in mid-December, I found ill in a field and brought home. For about ten days he lay sleepily curled up in a box of straw, refusing all food and drink. Then my wife and I having to go away for Christmas, he was left with hospitable friends who delighted us on our return with the news that the badger had roused himself and had decided very seasonably at Christmas that his fast was over and had forthwith devoured a succession of raw eggs and chunks of hare, pheasant and chicken.

So that by the time I got him back he was much livelier than before and accepted human company to the extent of taking food from my hand, including a piece of ginger cake which he munched with evident relish.

So he prospered: in fact better than I knew, as I discovered when I decided to house him in a pen as an improvement on his box. For then, misled by the traces of wheezings and twitchings he still had not quite got rid of, I greatly underestimated his strength. Next morning I found he had forced up the wire netting, staples and all, and decamped. And as it is only a field's length to his native wood I presume he returned to his kin. Or perhaps they came and fetched him?

My Longest Walk

Listening for foxes under the last full moon I found myself remembering the longest moonlight walk I ever did. I was then living in the Midlands and one day, it was December 31, a friend said: 'Let's go and walk across the border into Wales'. It was past midday when we arrived by train at Church Stretton but we were soon up and over Long Mynd and going as straight across country as lanes and tracks allowed. It was already deep dusk when we passed near Bishop's Castle and it was through strong moonlight that we climbed to the empty loneliness of Clun Forest. At midnight on Kerry Hill, and just inside Wales, we stopped in a sheltered hollow, made a great log fire and celebrated the New Year with a feast of Welsh rarebit. It must have been nearly 3 a.m. before we set off home. The moon was still bright, the air still and mild and our walk back over the hills had a strangely timeless, unreal quality for we were half asleep yet enjoying every mile. In daylight we faced the final testing trudge back over Long Mynd and so down again to Church Stretton after a walk of about 45 miles, half of which had been moon-aided. I doubt if long-distance hill walking by moonlight will ever be popular (though it did once have quite a vogue) but I recommend all who can to try it at least once.

Cage-bird Hypocrisy, 1970

Lately I heard that someone hereabouts possesses a captive quetzal. 'You ought to go and see it,' I was told, 'it's quite the most wonderful creature you ever saw.' I can believe it. The quetzal, Guatemala's national bird, is claimed to be the most beautiful bird in the world. I have its portrait before me at this minute. It is a dazzling green bird about the size of a cuckoo; its back is bright blue, its underparts red and white, and beyond its tail extend scintillating green plumes a couple of feet in length. If I liked to go only a few miles I could see this wonderful species in the flesh. But I shall not go. For I have just read a dismal snippet of news about quetzals: for every one successfully exported from South America there are fifty which die in transit.

Much the same can be said about most birds and animals caught for the world's cages: those which survive are a mere remnant of those originally caught. I remember reading an account by one zoo-animal catcher of how all the chimpanzees he caught in the Congo forests were dead before he could get them to the coast. (The man is now a famous television 'animal lover.') But to return to those wretched quetzals. Is it not quintessential hypocrisy for us to protect our own birds by law and yet go on importing the birds of other lands?

Massacre of the Oystercatchers, 1973

From time to time nature conservationists suffer major defeats. A few years ago we lost the battle of Cow Green and so a part of Upper Teesdale, in County Durham, with its botanical treasures, was flooded. This winter in Wales we have lost the battle of Burry Inlet and thousands of oystercatchers have been shot by permission of the Secretary of State for Wales and the Minister of Agriculture. Why? Because the birds are allegedly reducing the number of cockles in an area where cockling is a local industry. But if the cockles have declined, what proof is there that oystercatchers are responsible? It could be pollution of the water by the local tinplate factories. More likely it is because the cockles are being over-fished by man, just as whales are. There is another point. Even if oystercatchers are reducing the cockle population, will this shooting produce any reduction of oystercatchers in Burry Inlet? Will not their place be taken immediately by oystercatchers from less favourable feeding grounds? Who better than the Ministry of Agriculture to know that the shooting of woodpigeons is a futile exercise? And what about rabbits? In pre-myxomatosis Pembrokeshire millions of rabbits were trapped every year. But this only encouraged the rest to breed more enthusiastically to keep the numbers up. Surely it should have been proved conclusively that oystercatchers were responsible for a reduction in cockles before these horrible and probably futile killings were allowed? Whatever happened to British justice?

Rollicking Ravens

For us it is now the raven season. For though we see these splendid birds on and off all the year it is now that they appear in numbers. Strange in many ways, ravens are out of tune with the rest of nature, being always a season ahead. Early winter is their pairing time and by late winter they are building their great stick nests on rocks or trees. So in December we see them chasing each other wildly about the sky amid great croakings, barkings and gruntings. Life can never be dull as long as ravens are about. As pets they are famous entertainers and they are just as good in the wild, often making funny noises or up to something interesting. This morning I watched one coming over in a long, slow glide. Without warning he turned over on his back, uttered a loud, deep *pruk-pruk,* then righted himself. This he repeated every fifteen seconds, the notes always being uttered when he was upside down. Once he seemed so lost in the joy of flying upside down that he glided on for a dozen yards in that strange position. Finally, he flew slowly away making a noise like a stone dropped into a bucket every few seconds. Then he called in a ridiculous falsetto voice, pulled a few corks out of bottles, turned over three times in rapid succession and vanished by a sudden plunge into an oak-wood.

Walk in a Bronze Age Landscape

Christmas Day we devoted to the Bronze Age. Or, if you like, we went beating some of the bounds of our parish. Ours is an extremely tilted parish: for while one edge dangles in the estuary mud the other rises up steep grassy slopes and rocks to the highest point at 1,700 feet. It is up there that you find a perfect Bronze Age landscape with the parish boundary marked onward by cairn after cairn along the summit ridge. They look across a world of bleached grass and grey rocks to Cader Idris in the north and Pumlumon in the south, mountains that were doubtless of great significance to Bronze Age man. Nine or ten of these splendid piles of stones still survive, though it is 2,000 years since their makers heaped them over the remains of their most revered dead. The cairns evidently survive there because no one has ever had cause to build a wall on that particular ridge. Otherwise the stones would have been carried off long ago. Not that they have been left entirely untouched. All but one cairn have obviously been rifled by treasure hunters probably in recent times. But, what is rare, one of them seems intact for it is smoothly covered by turf. Long may it so remain. For though some cairns need to be opened for scientific reasons, one or two of these ancient graves should, I think, be left untouched even by archaeologists.

Rain-forest Tragedy, 1976

World shortages of pretty well everything (except people) suddenly seem to be coming at us from all directions. And only because we are so incredibly wasteful of absolutely everything. Take paper for instance. Even among conservationists how many of us make sure our waste paper goes back for re-cycling? The other day I heard a newspaper proprietor on the radio bemoaning the shortage of newsprint. It was forcing him to cut down the size of his paper. But so what? Except for the adverts his paper is only a daily stream of twaddle. And most of the adverts are trying to talk people into acquiring consumer goods they only buy because their money is burning a hole in their pockets. However, this newpaper owner saw brighter days ahead. He foresaw the newsprint situation being relieved quite soon now that the Brazilian Government has decided to clear the Amazon forest. Evidently the destruction of this unique forest with its vastly rich fauna and flora meant nothing to this individual. Nor will it mean anything to mankind in general. For despite all the lessons he has had about plundering the earth, man is quite unrepentant. Even as the end of oil comes in sight he moves in on another primal resource. Maybe if the Amazon forests were going to save us from some disaster, their exploitation might be justified. But all they are going to save us from is having to do without more and more trashy newspapers, tons of pornography, millions of pink forms in triplicate and so on. Man is undeniably very clever but he never, never learns.

Profits and Losses, 1983

Totting up the profit and loss account for 1983 I see from my diary that the year came in deliciously mild and that a bitter east wind in mid-February did not discourage the yellow gagea from flowering bravely at its only British locality, a limestone rock just within Wales. In March I walked the ridge of the Presely hills and looked across all Pembrokeshire. I failed to climb Snowdon in early April because the top 500 feet was a sheet of dangerous ice. In May the one rare plant in our parish, an orchid called narrow-leaved helleborine, produced only one flowering spike. It has long been declining and this looked like the end of the road.

In June, on a visit to sand-dunes in Anglesey, I was cheered to see the round-leaved wintergreen everywhere though when I knew it there years ago it was a hush-hush rarity. August brought us the clouded yellow butterfly and I was introduced to a pretty yellow migrant moth called the vestal. The highlight of September was a pure white swallow. That of October was a trip to Suffolk to see the true native black poplar and an ancient oak-wood full of medieval atmosphere. November was saddened by the death of Professor E. G. Bowen of Aberystwyth. He was not only a famous teacher of geography but also a scholar who wrote and lectured on an astonishing range of subjects. Yet, though so eminent, he was always just as ready to come and talk to a small village group as he was to address the Royal Society.

Choughs Ever a Delight

I was bending over some job in the garden the other day when I heard the faint cry of a bird high overhead. But though it came from far away it was perfectly distinctive, a sharp and cheerful jackdaw sort of cry but more musical than any jackdaw could hope to be. This bird was telling me so emphatically that it was a chough that I didn't even bother to look up. For most of my life I have lived in what might loosely be called chough country but the birds are so thin on the ground that to meet one is always a happy surprise. In fact, I don't suppose we have heard a chough over our garden more than three times in nearly thirty years. There are two unequal populations of choughs in Wales. The larger group lives on the coasts and islands while the smaller number is scattered inland, some of them being distinctly mountaineers. Indeed, the highest bird of any sort I have ever seen in Wales was a chough circling like an eagle far above the peak of Snowdon. It is these inland choughs which over the years have most brought me the pleasure of the unexpected bird. Usually they have simply flown over, helpfully calling out their name in a manner to be recommended to the whole world of birds. But there have been special days when they have fed on the ground quite tamely, giving me close views of their red legs and curved, red, slender beaks contrasting beautifully with their black plumage. In the air or on the ground, there are few birds more elegant than choughs.

The Wild Rocks of Arddu

On a rare sparkling day I explored the hills just south of Snowdon. On this side Snowdon plunges 3,000 feet into the vale of Gwynant which is graced by steep oak woodlands and two perfect lakes. From there the land climbs immediately to another realm of savage rocks, a region nothing like as high as Snowdon but, in these touristy days, far more wild and desolate. This is the land that rises into a chaos of cliffs, boulders, screes and lakelets above the east side of the Nanmor valley. Then far above, the long backbone of Cnicht stands high and alone, looking over all this alpine scene and far down Cardigan Bay. One way into this bony, barren land is by a footpath that sets off east from the head of the Nanmor valley and climbs without hesitation towards the craggy skyline. The prospects build up quickly all round and quite soon you are looking at mountains in every direction. Despite the rocks and peatbogs underfoot, the path goes bravely on, for this is one of the favourite ways to Cnicht and is not yet an outworn track like those up Snowdon, being neither grossly widened by too many boots nor turned into a porridge of trampled peat. You reach a shelf of grassy moorland and beyond it a deep-looking lake darkened by north-facing precipices. Now you are really getting into the barren upland called Yr Arddu which is made up of terrace above terrace of rough, grey rocks. In all Snowdonia there are few wildernesses quite like this ravined and crumpled landscape whose nakedness speaks so vividly of the ravages of geological time.

INDEX